JOYOUS JOURNEYS

AROUND THE DETOURS

JUANITA PURCELL

REGULAR BAPTIST
RBP Press

Quotations on pages 10, 40, 71, and 76 are from *Wholly Living* by John A. Huffman, Jr. © 1981; SP Publications, Inc., Wheaton, Ill. 60187. Published by Victor Books. Used by permission.

Quotations on pages 12 and 95 are from *Thru the Bible with J. Vernon McGee* by J. Vernon McGee. Used by permission of Thomas Nelson, Inc., Publishers. All rights reserved.

Quotations on pages 25, 47, 69, and 76 are from *Devotional Studies in Philippians* by Lehman Strauss. © 1959; Loizeaux, Neptune, N.J.; 1-800-526-2796. Used by permission.

Quotations on pages 26, 46, 66, and 84 are from *Bound for Joy* by Stuart Briscoe. © 1975; G/L Publications, Glendale, Calif. Used by permission.

Quotations on pages 38 and 39 are from *A Lamp for My Feet* by Elisabeth Elliot. © 1985 by Elisabeth Elliot. Servant Publications, Box 8617, Ann Arbor, Mich. 48107. Used by permission.

Quotations on pages 39 and 41 are from "Selected Illustrations from *Bible Illustrator.*" © 1990–91; Parsons Technology, Inc. All rights reserved. Used by permission.

Quotation on page 42 is from *If* by Amy Carmichael. © 1938; Christian Literature Crusade. Used by permission.

Quotations on pages 48 and 85 are from *My Utmost for His Highest* by Oswald Chambers. © 1935; Dodd, Mead & Co., renewed 1963 by the Oswald Chambers Publications Assn., Ltd. Used by permission of Discovery House Publishers, Box 3566, Grand Rapids, Mich. 49501. All rights reserved.

Quotation on page 53 is from *Mature Living,* May 1990. © 1990; The Sunday School Board of the Southern Baptist Convention. All rights reserved. Used by permission.

Quotations on pages 65, 79, 83, 84, 88, and 94 are from *Stand United in Joy: An Exposition of Philippians* by Robert Gromacki. © 1980; Baker Book House. Used by permission.

Quotations on pages 71 and 97 are from *From the Father's Heart* by Charles Slagle. © 1989; Charles Slagle. Used by permission of Destiny Image Publishers, P. O. Box 351, Shippensburg, Pa. 17257.

Quotation on page 73 is from *The Joy of Living* by J. Dwight Pentecost. © 1973; The Zondervan Corporation. Used by permission.

Every attempt was made to find the source for the story on page 98. Any information regarding the story will be acknowledged in future editions of this book.

Joyous Journeys around the Detours
© 1994
Regular Baptist Press • Arlington Heights, Illinois
www.RegularBaptistPress.org • 1-800-727-4440
Printed in U.S.A.
All rights reserved
RBP5219 • ISBN: 978-0-87227-182-1

Eleventh printing—2018

CONTENTS

A SPECIAL THANKS

To Tony Woolford for the great job he has done in advertising and marketing my books. He has given me encouragement that my books are meeting needs in ladies' lives.

PREFACE

Just days before I had planned to start writing this Bible study on the book of Philippians, I told a doctor and his wife, "You need to adopt my motto for this year: adjust or self-destruct." Little did I know that a week later the doctor would say to me, *"You* need to make some adjustments in *your* life." Without realizing it, I had stretched myself so far I was on the verge of burnout.

I spent the next two weeks in bed so my mind and body could unwind, relax, and get recharged. I read my Bible each day and kept my daily journal, but I did nothing else relating to ministry. I must have looked at every dress catalog, craft book, and catalog of any kind in the house. One day a lady called me and asked me how I was doing. I replied, "Just fine; I ordered 150 dresses today." She said, "Oh my, how are you ever going to pay for all of them?" I quickly assured her I had only been daydreaming.

Staying in bed those two weeks was like being in prison. Then I remembered that Paul said, while in prison, "I have learned, in whatsoever state I am, therewith to be content" (Philippians 4:11). Two verses later Paul wrote, "I can do all things through Christ which strengtheneth me." I serve the same God Paul served. If He did that for Paul, He could do it for me as well.

The biggest adjustment I had to make was giving up all my responsibilities for a few months. One week before, I had started teaching my evening and day Bible studies. We were studying my book, *Stretch My Faith, Lord.* The first lesson was on James 1:2–4, "Count it all joy when ye fall into [various trials]." It was a unique experience to hear others teach me the lessons I had written. That was an adjustment I was not ready to make, but learned to enjoy. Writing this book also had to be put on the back burner for a few months.

These were real detours in my plans. I had a choice to make: Would I joyously journey around the detours and adjust, or would I kick, scream and rebel, and self-destruct? I am learning to live out Philippians 4:13: "I can do all things through Christ which strengtheneth me." I am learning to be content with the detours and make the needed adjustments.

I've learned that the joy of the Lord does not depend on favorable circumstances in my life, but on a proper relationship with Christ. When my relationship with Christ is right, I can joyously accept the detours He sends into my life.

I trust this study will help you joyously journey around the detours in your life.

INTRODUCTION

Before we begin to study the book of Philippians, we need to know a few things about it.

Who wrote the book?

Paul identified himself as the writer in Philippians 1:1. (Timothy was with Paul in Rome [see Philippians 2:19], but Paul was the writer. Note the many times he used the singular pronoun "I.")

When was the book written?

Bible scholars date the writing of the book about A.D. 60.

To whom was it written?

Paul wrote to the "saints in Christ Jesus which are at Philippi" (Philippians 1:1).

What is the background of the book?

Paul visited Philippi on his second missionary journey (Acts 16:12) around A.D. 52. You may have a map in the back of your Bible that shows Paul's missionary journeys. If so, use that map to locate Philippi and the other places mentioned below.

Paul normally went first to the synagogue when he came into a city. However, not enough Jews were in Philippi to have a synagogue, so those who desired to worship gathered by a river where they could use the water for ceremonial rites. At that riverside Paul met Lydia, who became the first convert (Acts 16:14, 15). This was the beginning of the church at Philippi. The Philippian jailer and his family were soon added to the church (Acts 16:27–34).

On Paul's third missionary journey, he returned to the churches he had previously established—including the Philippian church—so he could nurture the believers. Paul concluded his journey in Jerusalem. There he was arrested (Acts 21:26–33). After two years, he was sent to Rome to appear before Caesar (Acts 24:27; 25:9–12; 28:16). Paul was a prisoner in Rome, but he was under "house arrest." He was confined to his house and was guarded by Roman soldiers

(Acts 28:16, 30). From this location Paul wrote the book of Philippians; thus it is known as one of Paul's prison epistles.

Why was the book written?

Paul wanted to thank the believers in the church in Philippi for the gift of money they had sent him. Epaphroditus, a member of the Philippian church, had brought the money. After he arrived in Rome, he suffered a serious illness, which almost cost him his life. He recovered (Philippians 2:25–30), and Paul sent him back to Philippi with this thank-you letter. Because Epaphroditus had given Paul a firsthand account of the conditions in the Philippian church, Paul wrote words of encouragement for the believers' spiritual progress and unity in the faith.

What is the theme of the book?

The theme is "joy regardless of circumstances," based on Paul's frequent use of the word "rejoice." It is summed up in Philippians 4:4—"Rejoice in the Lord alway: and again I say, Rejoice."

LESSON 1

From Sinner to Saint: What a Transformation!

*"Being confident of this very thing, that he which hath begun
a good work in you will perform it until the day
of Jesus Christ" (Philippians 1:6).*

A popular gospel chorus says, "He's [God's] still workin' on me to make me what I ought to be." Is that true in your life? It certainly has been true in my life! I think the apostle Paul would say that was true in his life as well.

In Philippians 1:6 Paul stated that when God begins a work in a person's heart, He never quits working on him until the day he goes to Heaven. When and where did God begin this work in Paul's heart and change him from a sinner to a saint? To find the answers, we need to go back to the book of Acts.

1. What was Paul's Hebrew name? Read Acts 9:11 and 13:9.

2. When we are first introduced to Saul in Acts, what had he just witnessed? Read Acts 7:58–60.

3. Saul was a devout Jew, a Pharisee, a leader in Judaism. Why did he take part in the death of Stephen, a Christian? Read Acts 8:1–3 and 9:1.

4. How was Saul changed from a man who killed Christians to one whose life was threatened for being a Christian? Read Acts 9:1–24.

9

> *"Human nature is not fixed and for this we should thank God day and night! We are still capable of change. We can become something other than what we are. By the power of the gospel the covetous man may become generous, the egotist lowly in his own eyes. The thief may learn to steal no more, the blasphemer to fill his mouth with praises unto God."[1]*

5. God got Saul's attention in a dramatic way (Acts 9:3, 4). What did the Lord have to do to get your attention before you responded to Him?

6. After God had Saul's attention, what did He say to him? Read Acts 26:14.

God may have been convicting Saul of his sin, or Saul may have seen the futility of his persecution of the church. Regardless, God had prepared him for this salvation experience.

> *"You don't become a Christian by osmosis. God acts through His Holy Spirit, to bring you to repentance and trust in Jesus Christ. He is the Initiator. If you are a believer, there was a beginning point."[2]*

7. Immediately following his conversion, what happened to Saul? Read Acts 9:8 and 9.

8. What did God ask Ananias to do? Read Acts 9:10–12.

9. Why was Ananias afraid to go? Read Acts 9:13 and 14.

10. What situation might you face that would be comparable to Ananias's situation? Describe your fears in such a setting.

11. How did the Lord calm Ananias's fears? Read Acts 9:15 and 16.

12. Ananias obeyed the Lord and went to Saul's house. What happened to Saul after Ananias laid his hands on him? Read Acts 9:17 and 18.

Bible scholars believe three years elapsed between Acts 9:21 and 22. During those three years, Paul was in the desert in Arabia. "Neither went I up to Jerusalem . . . but I went into Arabia, and returned again unto Damascus. Then after three years I went up to Jerusalem to see Peter . . ." (Galatians 1:17, 18). "It seems probable that vv. 22–25 [Acts 9] refer to Paul's labors in Damascus after his return from Arabia (Gal. 1:17). The 'many days' (v. 23) may represent the 'three years' of Gal. 1:18, which intervened between Paul's return to Damascus and his visit to Peter."[3]

Those three years in Paul's life may have been lonely ones, but they were necessary years of training. Paul learned to draw his strength from the Lord alone.

> *Many of God's people are called upon to withdraw into Arabia. Think of Arabia as places of silence and loneliness, desert places. When God changes everything in our lives, we may resent it. Yet once we can accept it, we find it is the very thing we needed to draw us closer to Christ.*

Following the three years in Arabia, Paul began his public ministry. If you have not read the introduction on pages 7 and 8, read it now so you will know what happened in Paul's life and what led to his being a Roman prisoner and writing a letter to the church in Philippi.

Read Philippians 1:1.

Paul—who once was Saul, the sinner who became a saint—addressed the readers of his book as "saints." The word "saint" is from the Greek word *hagioi,* which means "sanctified, set apart, holy."

13. The same word *hagioi,* or "saints," is used in 1 Corinthians 1:2. What did Paul say about saints in that verse?

> *"The human family is divided into two groups: the saints and the ain'ts. Saints are believers in Christ. They are saints, not because of their conduct, but because of their position in Christ. Saint means 'holy,' set apart for God. Anything that is holy is separated for the use of God. Even the old pots and pans in the tabernacle were called 'holy vessels,' and they were probably beaten and battered after forty years in the wilderness. They may not have looked holy, but they were. Why? Because they had been set aside for the use of God."*[4]

14. What other phrase did Paul use to describe saints in 2 Thessalonians 1:10?

15. Are saints select people who have received special recognition from God because of devoted service? No, that is not God's description of saints. Review your answers to questions 13 and 14 and write your definition of a saint.

How did Saul the sinner become Paul the saint? He came into a personal relationship with Jesus Christ because of the work God had begun in his heart (Philippians 1:6). Paul never planned to become a Christian; his plan was to kill Christians. But God interrupted his plans and initiated a good work in his heart. Paul was transformed!

> *"What we mean by salvation is this—deliverance from the love of sin, rescue from the habit of sin, setting free from the desire to sin."*[5]

16. What about you? Are you a saint, one who has experienced God's salvation? Are you positive that if you died today you would go to Heaven? If your answer is yes, describe your salvation experience.

If you are not sure of your salvation, read the verses that follow.

God **loves** you and wants you to enjoy the **abundant life** He offers you.

John 3:16—"For God so loved the world, that he gave his only begotten Son, that whosoever believeth in him should not perish, but have everlasting life."

John 10:10—"I am come that they might have life, and that they might have it more abundantly."

Man is **sinful,** and his sin **separates** him from God.

Romans 3:23—"For all have sinned, and come short of the glory of God."

Romans 6:23—"For the wages of sin is death [spiritual separation from God]. . . ."

Jesus Christ's death is the only **provision** God has made to pay for man's sin.

Romans 5:8—"But God commendeth his love toward us, in that, while we were yet sinners, Christ died for us."

John 14:6—"Jesus saith unto him, I am the way, the truth, and the life: no man cometh unto the Father, but by me."

You must **receive** Jesus Christ as your Savior before you can personally experience His love for you and the abundant life He has planned for you.

John 1:12—"But as many as received him, to them gave he power to become the sons of God, even to them that believe on his name."

You can invite Christ into your life right now by a simple act of **faith.**

Ephesians 2:8—"For by grace are ye saved through faith. . . ."

Are you ready to invite Christ into your life to be your Savior? Use the following prayer as a guide to help you express your desire to God: "Lord Jesus, thank You for dying on the cross for my sins. Right now I open my heart and invite You into my life as my Savior. Thank You for forgiving my sin and giving me everlasting life. I want You to have control of my life so I can experience the abundant life You have planned for me."

The Bible **promises eternal life** to all who receive Christ as Savior.

1 John 5:11–13—"And this is the record, that God hath given to us eternal life, and this life is in his Son. He that hath the Son hath life; and he that hath not the Son of God hath not life. These things have I written unto you that believe on the name of the Son of God; that ye may know that ye have eternal life, and that ye may believe on the name of the Son of God."

Did you invite Christ into your life? You can be sure you

have eternal life based on 1 John 5:11–13. To help you always remember this exciting experience in your life, write in the front of your Bible, "Today (date) I invited Christ into my life to be my Savior." I also encourage you to share with your Bible study leader what has happened to you. I, too, would like to know of your salvation and would like to send you a booklet that will help you in living for Christ. Please write to me in care of the publisher of this book.

 ## *From My Heart*

How long has it been since you rehearsed your salvation experience? I asked you to do that in this lesson, and I would like to share my experience with you.

It was a Sunday evening many, many years ago, in a little country church in Mount Vernon, Illinois. I was with my boyfriend (who is now my husband, J.O.). I went to church Sunday mornings, Sunday evenings, and Wednesday evenings—not so much to be in church, but to be with my boyfriend.

On that Sunday evening we were sitting in the back of the church with the other teens. We were singing the closing song, and the pastor was inviting people to come forward to receive Christ. I saw J.O.'s father walking to the back of the church. This seemed unusual because he always sat on the front pew. I soon realized he was coming to talk to me. "Little Lady (he always called me "Little Lady"), wouldn't you like to get saved tonight?" Before I knew what was happening, I said yes and was walking to the front of the church. We got down on our knees by that front pew, and I invited Christ into my life to be my personal Savior.

Little did that teenager realize she had become a "saint," and never in my wildest dreams could I have imagined what special mission God had planned for my life. When God called my husband into the ministry, I fought God's convicting ministry in my life for five years. Finally, one day I got down on my knees in my dining room and, like Paul, said, "Lord, what wilt Thou have me to do?"

I'm so glad God didn't give up on me! He just kept working on me until I was willing to obey and answer His call. What God starts, He always finishes—*He is so faithful!*

From Your Heart

Thank God for the work He has done and is doing in your life. Share your "transformation story" with someone this week.

Notes

1. A. W. Tozer, quoted by G. B. Smith, compiler, *Renewed Day by Day* (Grand Rapids: Baker Book House, 1980), April 19.

2. John A. Huffman, Jr., *Wholly Living* (Wheaton, Ill.: Victor Books, 1981), p. 9.

3. Note on Acts 9:22, *The New Scofield Study Bible,* p. 1327.

4. J. Vernon McGee, *Thru the Bible with J. Vernon McGee* (Nashville: Thomas Nelson, Inc., Publishers, 1983), vol. 5, p. 289.

5. Tom Carter, compiler, *Spurgeon at His Best* (Grand Rapids: Baker Book House, 1988), p. 179.

LESSON 2
Gratitude or Grumbling?
PHILIPPIANS 1:1–11

"I thank my God upon every remembrance of you"
(Philippians 1:3).

Paul wrote the book of Philippians while he was a Roman prisoner. In spite of his situation, he wrote, "I have learned, in whatsoever state I am, therewith to be content" (Philippians 4:11). Paul learned to be joyful and content in all kinds of conditions and circumstances.

How can our lives be filled with joy in spite of our circumstances? To answer this question, consider these three words: Christ, mind, joy. Paul used these words repeatedly in the book of Philippians.

Christ, Lord Jesus, Jesus Christ—36 times
Mind—11 times
Joy or rejoice—16 times

How can we have joy in spite of our circumstances? The same way Paul did: by keeping our minds on Christ and not on circumstances. The way we think determines the way we act and react. Someone once said, "Your attitude determines your altitude." Remember, joy is offered to "saints," God's children. Did you get that settled in lesson 1?

Precious memories are a cause for gratitude.
Read Philippians 1:1–5.

1. Why did Paul mention Timothy's name in his greeting to the church (verse 1)? Skim Acts 16:1—17:15 and read Philippians 2:19.

2. To whom does the word "bishops" refer in verse 1? Read
   1 Timothy 3:1–7.

Paul began all his letters to churches with the saluta-
tion, "grace and peace" (verse 2). The Greek word for grace,
charis, was a word of greeting in the Greek world. The
Greeks used *charis* as we would say, "Have a good day."
"Peace" *(shalom)* is a Hebrew form of greeting.
    Paul knew the Philippian church wasn't perfect, but he
had happy memories when he thought of his relationship
with these people.

3. Paul exhibited a thankful heart—even in prison (verse
   3). People with grateful hearts are content. On the con-
   trary, ungrateful people are subject to discontentment,
   bitterness, and complaining. In which category are you?
   If you are ungrateful, how can you change? Read Philippians 4:11 and 13.

---

*"The grateful person feels a great sense of un-
worthiness—'I have so much more than I deserve.' But an ungrateful person feels, 'I deserve
so much more than I have.' "*[1]

---

4. What could Paul have remembered about the Philippians
   (verse 3) that brought joy to his heart? Read Acts 16:14,
   15, and 23–34.

---

*"Memory! What a world in a word! According to
the poets, memory is given so we might have
summer roses right through winter. Aristotle aptly
described memory as the 'scribe of the soul.'
Memory is one of God's great gifts to human-
kind."*[2]

---

5. Paul prayed for the Philippians (verse 4), as well as for many other people. (See, for example, Romans 1:8–10, Ephesians 1:16–23, and Colossians 1:3.) (a) What characterized Paul's prayer for the Philippians?

(b) Why do you think he was able to pray this way?

6. How did the Philippians share ("fellowship," verse 5) with Paul in the spread of the gospel? Read Philippians 4:15 and 16 and 2 Corinthians 8:1–4.

Confidence in Christ is a cause for gratitude.
Read Philippians 1:6–11.

7. Of what was Paul confident (verse 6)?

8. Why is confidence in God so important for the Christian? Read 2 Corinthians 5:7.

9. When we fail to have confidence in God, we lose our joy. What are some things that rob us of joy and confidence in God?

> " 'Loving life and seeing good days' seems little
> more than an elusive pipe dream for too many of
> God's children. One reason is because we allow
> kill-joys to come in. Yes, kill-joys. We allow cer-
> tain attitudes and practices to become attached to
> our Christianity like barnacles on a ship. These
> barnacles suck the life out of our Christianity and
> kill off our joy." [3]

10. The Greek verb translated "begun" in verse 6 is also
    used in Galatians 3:3. What good work had God begun in
    these believers' lives?

11. The faithful God Who started our salvation will com-
    plete, or finish, it. What does He want the finished prod-
    uct to look like? Read Romans 8:29.

> "What comforts me is the thought that we are
> being shaped here below into stones for the heav-
> enly temple,—that to be made like Him is the
> object of our earthly existence. He is the shaper
> and carpenter of the heavenly temple. He must
> work us into shape; our part is to be still in His
> hands." [4]

12. We can be confident that God never gives up on us. He
    just keeps hammering, banging, and sanding away. How
    long will He keep working on us (verse 6)?

13. What is the "day of Jesus Christ"? Read 1 Thessalonians
    4:16–18 and 1 John 3:2.

"What a dreary journey would this be if we did not have that last page in the Book! There is so much now that defies explanation. But one day every- thing will be fixed and final. . . . Things do not add up now but one day the facts will all be in, the accounts settled without appeal. Everything and everybody will be where they belong. Don't live for today. Live for that last page!"[5]

14. Having confidence that God is finishing His work in our own lives will bring gratitude and joy. But Paul also had confidence regarding the Lord's working in the Philip- pians' lives. How could verse 6, along with Philippians 2:13, be an encouragement when a loved one is not walk- ing with the Lord?

15. What was Paul expressing when he said, "I have you in my heart" (verse 7)?

16. Paul's love for the Philippians was more than mere hu- man interest. Where did Paul's love originate (verse 8)?

17. As Paul prayed with confidence in God for the Philippian believers, what three specific requests did he make?
    Verse 9

    Verse 10

Verse 11

18. Why do you think Paul put abounding love at the top of his prayer list? Read Galatians 5:22 and 1 Corinthians 13:13.

19. Paul's prayer for the Philippians is one we can use for friends and family. For whom could you pray the words of verses 9–11?

 From My Heart

If I asked you, "Do you have a prayer list?" you would probably say yes. You may have it written down on paper or written in your heart, as Paul did ("I have you in my heart"— verse 7). You may also have a praise list, recording answers to prayer. But do you have a thanksgiving list? I didn't have one until I wrote this lesson. I realized Paul's happy memories of God's faithfulness in the past helped him to be filled with joy in his present circumstances. I decided to reflect on the past forty years in my journey with Christ. I then made my thanksgiving list. Needless to say, I placed my salvation at the top of the list.

Why have a thanksgiving list? When the hard times come, you can get out your list and rehearse all the things for which you are thankful. "Count your blessings, name them one by one, And it will surprise you what the Lord has done." You won't have much time left to think about your present, unpleasant circumstances. Try it! I did. It works!

From Your Heart

Is your life marked by grumbling or gratitude? Start making your thanksgiving list today.

Notes

1. Nancy Leigh DeMoss, "The Attitude of Gratitude," *Spirit of Revival* (Nov. 1992), p. 5.

2. Henry Gariepy, *Portraits of Perseverance* (Wheaton, Ill.: Victor Books, 1989), p. 97.

3. David Warren, "Are You a Happy Christian?" *Cedarville Torch* (Spring 1993), p. 7.

4. Charles George Gordon, quoted by Mary Wilder Tileston, *Joy and Strength* (Minneapolis: World Wide Publications, 1929), p. 55.

5. Vance Havner, *Though I Walk through the Valley* (Old Tappan, N.J.: Fleming H. Revell Co., 1974), p. 59.

Confidence in Christ, No Matter What!

PHILIPPIANS 1:12–26

"For to me to live is Christ, and to die is gain"
(Philippians 1:21).

Contented, grateful, praising God—yet sitting in prison! Our minds say, "Impossible!" Yet we see from Paul's life it is not impossible. In fact, we will learn in this lesson that this attitude is possible if we develop Paul's philosophy of life: "For to me to live is Christ, and to die is gain" (Philippians 1:21).

This is not some pie-in-the-sky dream for saints shut away in monasteries; it is for modern-day saints in the twenty-first century. Let's find out how it can become a reality in our lives.

In lesson 1 we learned that Paul had absolute confidence in Christ regarding his salvation and life in Christ. In this lesson we will see that Paul was confident in three other areas: confident in trying circumstances; confident in the face of death; confident in daily life.

Confident in trying circumstances
Read Philippians 1:12–20.

Paul was imprisoned, but his prison did not have iron bars. His imprisonment was very unusual. "And when we came to Rome, the centurion delivered the prisoners to the captain of the guard: but Paul was suffered [permitted] to dwell by himself with a soldier that kept him" (Acts 28:16). Paul's situation was not as bad as it could have been, but being chained to a guard twenty-four hours a day would not be pleasant, no matter what the setting might be.

24

1. Instead of complaining about his situation, Paul expressed joy about what was accomplished because of his difficult circumstances. What was happening? Read verses 12 and 13.

"Paul in prison. That was another side of life. Do you want to see how he takes it? I see him looking out over the top of his prison wall and over the heads of his enemies. I see him write a document and sign his name—not the prisoner of Festus, nor of Caesar; not the victim of the Sanhedrin; but the—'prisoner of the Lord.' He saw only the hand of God in it all. To him the prison becomes a palace. Its corridors ring with shouts of triumphant praise and joy."[1]

---

2. How did Paul's response to his adverse circumstances affect other believers? Read verses 14 and 18.

"The advantage that life's limitations can have in my personal life is a matter which only I can decide. If I whine and wince under the circumstances, I am shriveling my own soul and showing a shallowness of Christian experience. If I can be content and remain consistent above the circumstances, I help myself and others."[2]

---

3. Paul rejoiced that the gospel was being preached, but some people were preaching from false motives (verses 15–17). What were their motives?

4. What was Paul's attitude toward his critics (verse 18)?

> *"Paul may have learned from Stephen that what happens to us when people hurt us won't matter years from now unless we have chosen to carry the resentful memory of it like a dead weight through life. But a forgiving spirit sheds that weight and springs us free. . . ."[3]*

5. Paul responded with joy to imprisonment and to personal attacks and criticism. (a) How do we usually react when we are criticized?

   (b) What did Christ say our response should be? Read Matthew 5:44.

6. What confidence did Paul express in verse 19? The word "salvation" may be translated "release" or "deliverance." Also read Philippians 2:24.

7. Paul could see his imprisonment as part of God's plan for his life. Looking back at a time of testing in your life, how do you see it as a part of God's plan for you?

> *"Paul had more than his share of disappointment, not least his imprisonment, but he had learned that disappointment can be His-appointment."[4]*

8. What great desire did Paul express in verse 20?

9. Think about what a magnifying lens does. (a) What did Paul mean by magnifying Christ in his body?

(b) How do 1 Corinthians 6:20 and 10:31 relate to Philippians 1:20?

10. Do you have the kind of confidence in Christ that you can say to Him, "Give what You want, take what You want; I want You to be magnified in my body"? If so, how is this confidence shown?

Confident in the face of death
Read Philippians 1:21–24.

11. How would you finish this sentence: "For me, real living is or would be . . ."?

12. What did Paul mean when he said, "For to me to live is Christ"? How did Paul describe his Christian life in Galatians 2:20?

13. What would Paul gain by dying? Read 2 Corinthians 5:8.

14. Christ was at the center of Paul's life. Look at the circles below and decide which one typifies your life.

Christ is the center of my life. My life revolves around what He wants for my life.

"Me" is the center of my life. My life revolves around what I want for myself.

15. Verse 21 ends with the words "and to die is gain." This part of the verse can only be true in our lives if the first part of the verse is true. Why is death loss if Christ is not the center of our lives? Read 2 Corinthians 5:8–10 and 1 John 2:28 as you consider your answer.

16. Paul said he was "hard pressed" between two things (verses 23, 24). What were they?

17. Paul was willing to live if that was God's choice for him. But he saw death as something "far better" (verse 23). Why did he have that view?

18. Paul was not afraid of death. Why do some believers fear death?

> Afraid? Of what?
> To feel the spirit's glad release?
> To pass from pain to perfect peace?
> The strife and strain of life to cease?
> > Afraid—of that?
>
> Afraid? Of what?
> Afraid to see the Savior's face?
> To hear His welcome, and to trace
> The glory gleam from wounds of grace?
> > Afraid—of that?
>
> Afraid? Of what?
> To enter into Heaven's rest?
> And yet to serve the Master blest,
> From service good to service best?
> > Afraid—of that?[5]

Confident in daily living
Read Philippians 1:25 and 26.

19. Paul knew the easiest way out of his adversities was death, but at this point he was confident he would live. Why?

20. Have you ever faced a circumstance so difficult that you felt the only way out was for Christ to take you Home? What gave you courage to face the circumstance and accept God's will?

 From My Heart

Few of us have circumstances as difficult as Paul's, but we all have trials. We can become prisoners to our circumstances if we let our minds dwell on them.

I once heard a nurse ask a patient, "Do you know how to control your pain?"

This question got my attention, and I said, "I didn't know we could control our pain."

The nurse explained that the basic idea was to choose an object to think about. This is what ladies do in Lamaze childbirth classes. They learn to think on an object and to breathe deeply. When the labor pains start, they focus their minds on something other than the pain. The nurse said she kept her mind on a gold necklace while she was in labor. The necklace had the names of her other children on it.

I said, "Wow! That's a perfect picture of Isaiah 26:3— 'Thou wilt keep him in perfect peace, whose mind is stayed on thee: because he trusteth in thee.' "

Ladies, have you learned that what you think about reveals what you are, and your thoughts predict what you will become? Our emotions follow our thinking. The best way to control our thoughts is to keep them centered on Christ. I'm trying to do that, but I fail so often. However, I'm not giving up! Remember, practice makes perfect! I want that perfect peace that God promises I can have. I want to have confidence in Christ regardless of my circumstances. Do you?

From Your Heart

Think again about your answer to question 11. How does your answer affect the way you handle the difficult times in life? What steps can you take this week to make Christ the center of your life?

Notes

1. Mrs. Charles E. Cowman, *Streams in the Desert—1* (Grand Rapids: Zondervan Publishing House, 1965), p. 269.

2. Lehman Strauss, *Devotional Studies in Philippians* (Neptune, N.J.: Loizeaux Brothers, 1959), p. 66.

3. Gail McDonald, *Keep Climbing* (Wheaton, Ill.: Tyndale House Publishers, 1989), pp. 84, 85.

4. Stuart Briscoe, *Bound for Joy* (Glendale, Calif.: G/L Publications, 1975), p. 22.

5. E. H. Hamilton.

The Remedy for Discord
PHILIPPIANS 1:27—2:4

*"Let nothing be done through strife or vainglory;
but in lowliness of mind let each esteem other
better than themselves" (Philippians 2:3).*

In Philippians 1:1–26 Paul talked about his own experiences. Now the focus changes to the experiences of the believers in the church at Philippi. Paul began by talking about their conduct and attitude toward one another.

Evidently there was some disunity in the church, because Paul referred to being of one mind, or the same mind in chapters 1, 2, and 4. In fact, he even mentioned two women in particular who needed to be of the same mind: Euodias and Snytyche (4:2).

To make sure we get the full impact of Paul's message, we need to understand the meaning of the words "conversation" and "becometh." The old English word "conversation" meant "conduct, way of life, or behavior pattern," *not* "talk." The Greek word translated "conversation" is the word from which we get our word "politics" and has to do with the idea of citizenship. "Becometh" means "to be of equal weight." We could paraphrase the first part of verse 27 like this, "Make sure that your behavior, as citizens, adds up to the Christ you know and the gospel you present." In other words, our lives should be becoming to Jesus Christ.

Live as becometh the gospel.
Read Philippians 1:27–30.

1. Our manner of life as Christians either helps or hinders the gospel. What conduct of a believer is dishonoring to Christ?

31

> We are the only Bible
> The careless world will read;
> We are the sinner's gospel,
> We are the scoffer's creed;
> We are the Lord's last message,
> Given in deed and word;
> What if the type is crooked?
> What if the print is blurred?[1]

2. Paul hoped to visit the believers in Philippi; but if he couldn't, he wanted to hear good things about them. What particular thing did he want to hear (verse 27)?

3. Why do we tend to be slack in our behavior when we think others are not watching our lives?

4. Can we live our lives without being seen? Read Psalm 139:7 and 12. What effect should these verses have on what we do and say?

5. Paul wanted the believers in Philippi to practice steadfast living ("stand fast"). He repeated this command in Philippians 4:1; he also used it in some of his other letters. What areas of steadfast living are mentioned in the following verses?

   1 Corinthians 16:13

   Galatians 5:1

   2 Thessalonians 2:15

6. (a) Read verse 28. What do our adversaries try to do to us?

(b) Who is our main adversary? Read 1 Peter 5:8.

"Satan, the accuser of the saints, takes great delight in worrying feeble believers who sigh when they should be singing."[2]

---

7. Why do believers in Jesus Christ not have to be afraid of their adversaries? Read Romans 8:33–37.

8. Read verse 29 and 2 Timothy 3:12. What can a believer expect to experience?

9. What is the difference between experiencing the trials of life and suffering for Christ's sake?

> If all were easy, if all were bright,
> Where would the cross be, and where the fight?
> But in the hardness, God gives to you
> Chances of proving that you are true.[3]

10. What suffering did the Philippians see Paul experience (verse 30)? Read Acts 16:19–34.

Live in unity.
Read Philippians 2:1–4.

Chapter 2 begins with Paul's appeal for unity among the believers. Paul wanted the believers to keep bringing joy to his life, as they had before (Philippians 1:4–6), by their Christ-like living.

11. In verse 1 the word "if" can be translated "since" or "in view of the fact." Paul based his appeal for unity among the believers on four things they had experienced in their relationship with Christ. What were they?

12. What command did Paul give in verse 2?

13. What three things contribute to like-mindedness?

> To love the whole world
> For me is no chore;
> My only real problem's
> My neighbor next door.[4]

14. What does "being of one accord, of one mind" mean?

15. What causes discord instead of "one accord" (verse 3)?

16. Look up the words "strife" and "vainglory" in a dictionary. After you define the words, describe how each one can cause discord.
    Strife

    Vainglory

17. In verses 3 and 4 Paul gave two antidotes for strife and vainglory. What are they? Also read 1 Peter 5:5 and Romans 15:1 and 2.

"Self-preoccupation, self-broodings, self-interest, self-love,—these are the reasons why you go jarring against your fellows. Turn your eyes off yourself. . . . Look up and out, from this narrow, cabined self of yours, and . . . you will provoke no more; but you will, to your own glad surprise, find the secret of 'the meekness and the gentleness of Jesus'; and the fruits of the Spirit will all bud and blossom from out of your life."[5]

---

18. We hear and read about the importance of a proper self-image. What do verses 3 and 4 teach us about a Biblical view of self-image? Also read Matthew 20:26 and 27.

 From My Heart

Have you ever asked yourself the question, Who controls me? When I let the actions of others determine my reactions, I am controlled by every person I meet. How can I break this miserable habit that binds me? I must change my mind about myself. I must quit thinking about self and start thinking more of others. I must stop being so self-centered and self-protective.

I want to be *Spirit*-controlled, not *others*-controlled, don't you? Here are some steps to achieve that goal:

• Admit that my reactions have revealed how self-centered I am.

• Refuse to excuse and defend my actions.

• Confess my sin of self-centeredness.

• Live by Philippians 2:3—"In lowliness of mind let each esteem other better than themselves."

"Lord, help me to remember that You love to dwell in a quiet and peaceable heart. Strife and vainglory will hinder me from seeing You and sensing Your presence, even when You are beside me and trying to speak to me."

From Your Heart

Is there discord in your marriage or with a child, family member, or church member? List three things you could do for your spouse, child, family, friend. Pray about each item on your list, then do it. What do you think the result will be?

Notes

1. Annie Johnson Flint, quoted by Al Bryant, compiler, *Favorite Poems* (Grand Rapids: Zondervan, 1957), p. 13.

2. Dennis J. Hester, compiler, *The Vance Havner Quotebook* (Grand Rapids: Baker Book House, 1986), p. 201.

3. Gariepy, p. 154.

4. C. W. Vanderbergh, quoted by George Sweeting, *Love Is the Greatest* (Chicago: Moody Press, 1974), p. 94.

5. Henry Scott Holland, quoted by Tileston, p. 160.

LESSON 5

To Serve or Be Served?

PHILIPPIANS 2:5–11

"Let this mind be in you, which was also in Christ Jesus"
(Philippians 2:5).

In Philippians 2:1–4 Paul told the Philippians—and believers of our day—to get along with each other. But our sinful nature always causes us to defend our actions: "But you don't know Molly Jones! Getting along with her is an impossibility. She is so critical, rude, and just plain obnoxious. How in the world can I get along with her?"

Paul's answer might have been something like this, "I'm glad you asked! If you really want a good illustration of what I mean by looking out for the interests of others and getting along with them, look at Jesus Christ's example. He had everything, yet He gave it all up and became a servant. Yes, Christ is God, but He did not count equality with the Father as something He had to selfishly hang on to. He emptied Himself and made Himself of no reputation. He humbled Himself and became obedient unto the death of the cross."

What love! What a serving, humble spirit! That's the kind of loving spirit God wants us to have toward one another. When we have this kind of spirit, we can look beyond a person's faults and see her need.

A caring Christian has a humble, serving spirit. This lesson will help us learn how to develop that kind of spirit.

The attitude of a servant
Read Philippians 2:5–7.

1. Paul said believers should have "this mind," which was also the mind the Lord Jesus had. What is "this mind"? Refer to verses 3 and 4.

2. How did Christ display lowliness of mind, thinking of others ahead of Himself (verses 6 and 7)?

"If you want to be a Christian, see that your mind is made up as his was: be humble, be subject, be obedient—even to death. It will mean death. Be sure of that. Death to some of your desires and plans at least. Death to yourself."[1]

Verse 6 affirms the deity of Christ. He is the express image of God (Hebrews 1:3). "Robbery" means "something to be grasped or held by force." "Christ did not consider His existing in a manner equal to God as something to be held on to and used for His advantage."[2]

3. How does verse 6 relate to the principles expressed in verses 3 and 4?

In verse 7 "made himself of no reputation" means "emptied himself." Christ was still God—He never emptied Himself of His deity. He divested Himself of His self-interests. "He emptied Himself of the privileges and rights He had because He was God."[3]

4. When Christ emptied Himself, He laid aside all the privileges of Heaven. What are some things He gave up?

5. When did this "emptying" take place in Christ's life?

6. What must we do to be emptied of self? Read Matthew 16:24–26.

> *"To be transformed into the image of Christ I must learn his character, love his obedience to the will of the Father, and begin, step by step, to walk the same pathway. For Christ the pathway of obedience began with emptying Himself. I must begin at the same place."*[4]

7. Christ emptied Himself and became man. What "form" did He take (verse 7)?

8. What is your attitude toward serving others?

9. If we are to have the mind, or attitude, of Christ, what should be our attitude toward serving others? Read Matthew 20:28.

The actions of a servant
Read John 13:1–5, 14–17.

10. On the eve of Christ's death, what unusual thing did He do to help His disciples realize the importance of serving?

11. What did Christ want the disciples to learn from His actions (John 13:14)?

12. What do you think it means in our society today to wash one another's feet?

> You know, Lord, how I serve You
> with great emotional fervor in the limelight.
> You know how eagerly I speak for You at a Women's
>   Club.
> You know my genuine enthusiasm at a Bible study.

But how would I react, I wonder,
if You pointed to a basin of water
and asked me to wash the calloused feet
of a bent and wrinkled old woman
day after day, month after month,
in a room where nobody saw and nobody knew?[5]

13. Our society asks, "How high are you? What is your position?" Christ asks, "Are you washing one another's feet? How low are you?" What areas of service in the church could be considered "lowly"?

14. Think of someone you have a hard time loving. How would you react if someone asked you to wash that person's feet? What should be your reaction?

15. Review Philippians 2:3. What stops us from being willing to accept the role of servant?

> "What it all boils down to is that we are called to be servants. Ouch! Servants? Who wants to be a servant?... Would you like to be like Jesus Christ? ... He was a servant. He gave Himself for others. ... How quickly we forget our calling to be servants. How absorbed we become in our own self-interests. How insensitive we become to the needs of others while seeking to satisfy our own. Yet what joy, what wholeness of life we bring both to others and to ourselves when we faithfully carry out the attitudes and practices of servanthood. And what joy awaits us when we hear the wonderful words of our Lord, 'Well done, good and faithful servant' (Matt. 25:21)."[6]

True humility
Read Philippians 2:8–11.

16. Christ is the ultimate example of humility. How low did the Lord Jesus stoop (verse 8)?

17. (a) How does a believer with a humble spirit relate to God? Read James 4:10 and 1 Peter 5:6.

    (b) How does a humble believer think of herself? Read Romans 12:3.

    (c) How does a humble spirit show in her relationships with others? Read Romans 12:10.

"A young artist submitted one of his works to be hung in a prestigious art exhibit, but the selection committee rejected it. One of its members, however, the renowned landscape painter Joseph Turner, insisted that they include the young man's work. The others denied his plea, saying that there was simply no room for it. Turner said no more but quietly removed one of his own pictures, replacing it with that of the budding young artist."[7]

---

18. What does Luke 14:11 mean? Read also Proverbs 25:6 and 7 and James 4:10.

19. Because Christ willingly humbled Himself, what did the Father do? Read Philippians 2:9.

20. To what extent will Christ's name be known above every other name (verses 10, 11)?

 From My Heart

If someone asked you whom you used as a model for your life, I assume you would say, "Jesus Christ." But do you have an earthly model as well, someone who motivates you and challenges you spiritually?

Some years ago I heard about a missionary to India, Amy Carmichael. Something about this lady's love and dedication to Christ and others fascinated and challenged me. Then I read the biography of her life, *A Chance to Die,* written by Elisabeth Elliot. After reading the book, I understood the reason for the title. Never have I read of a woman who was so totally emptied of self as she was. Truly she had learned what it means to die daily to self and to be filled with the Holy Spirit. Amy Carmichael is one of my models. I'm sure I will never measure up to her or Jesus Christ, but I still try to fashion my life after these great models.

To give you a glimpse of Amy's heart, I will conclude with some thoughts from her book with the simple and striking title *If.*

> IF the praise of man elates me and
>   his blame depresses me;
> if I cannot rest under misunderstand-
>   ing without defending myself;
> if I love to be loved more than
>   to love,
> to be served more than to serve,
> then I know nothing of Calvary love.[8]

If I could be filled with Calvary love more than I am filled with *me*, I could make a difference in this world like Amy did.

From Your Heart

Do you focus on serving others or on having others serve you? What do you need to do to develop more of a servant spirit? Ask God to help you start today!

Notes

1. Elisabeth Elliot, *A Lamp for My Feet* (Ann Arbor, Mich.: Servant Publications, 1985), p. 39.

2. William Arp, *The Joyful Life* (Schaumburg, Ill.: Regular Baptist Press, 1994), teacher's guide, p. 38.

3. Arp, p. 38.

4. Elliot, p. 29.

5. Ruth Harms Calkin, quoted in "Selected Illustrations from *Bible Illustrator*" (Parsons Technology, Inc., 1990–91).

6. Huffman, pp. 46–48.

7. "Selected Illustrations from *Bible Illustrator*"

8. Amy Carmichael, *If* (Fort Washington, Pa.: Christian Literature Crusade, 1938), p. 60.

LESSON 6

So What If I Murmur and Complain?

PHILIPPIANS 2:12–18

"Do all things without murmurings and disputings"
(Philippians 2:14).

Philippians 2:5–11 pictures the humble, servant's attitude we can have when the mind of Christ dominates our lives. This next section of verses reminds us that we not only need to think right about ourselves, but we also need to act right.

The world is watching those who call themselves "Christians." We don't need to wear a name tag printed "CHRISTIAN"; we just need to live different. How different? Different enough that others will know we are Christians, Christlike ones! Hugh Black describes it like this: "The Christian life must be in its own degree something like the Master's own life, luminous with His hope, and surrounded by a bracing atmosphere which uplifts all who even touch its outer fringe."

God's work is inward.
Read Philippians 2:12 and 13.

1. Paul's presence could no longer be the motive for the Philippians' obedience. What motive did Paul give? Review Philippians 2:5–11.

Verse 12 talks about "working out" our salvation. We need to understand what that means.

2. What did you learn in Philippians 1:6 about your salvation? Also read Ephesians 2:8 and 9.

In Philippians 2:12 Paul spoke to believers, "my beloved." So "work out your own salvation" cannot mean to work *for* one's salvation. The verb translated "work out" carried the meaning of "work to full completion." An illustration of this is working out a math problem to full completion to get the answer.

3. With this meaning in mind, what do you think Paul meant by "work out your own salvation"?

"Working out salvation is somewhat similar to working out a marriage. Like marriage, salvation involves a lifetime of discovery and development. A married person knows he is married, but he ought to live like a married person."[1]

---

4. God wants His children to become grown-up, mature Christians. (a) What is the work God does in us (verse 13)? Read Romans 8:29.

(b) What is our work? Read Romans 12:1.

"In the divine order, God's working depends upon our co-operation. . . . Just as the potter, however skillful, cannot make a beautiful vessel out of a lump of clay that is never put into his hands, so neither can God make out of me a vessel unto His honor unless I put myself into His hands."[2]

---

5. Paul gave a distinct directive in verse 12 about how our salvation is to be worked out. What is it?

6. Because salvation is a free gift (John 3:16; Romans 6:23), some Christians see it as license for careless living. How will an attitude of fear and trembling affect the way we live out our salvation before others?

7. Without Christ, we would be weak and powerless to live the Christian life. How does verse 13 reassure us that the power is available?

"When God in Christ entered your life at the moment of your commitment to Him, you took on new significance. You were no longer little old you against the big cold world. You became little old you, the residence of the mighty, eternal God. *Little old you and the mighty, eternal God sharing one body, one life, one world and one society. What do you think could happen to your life and your world as a result?"[3]*

---

8. The Greek word translated "worketh in you" (verse 13) is the source of the English word "energy." For what does God energize us?

9. God works in us to make us willing to do His will. (a) Can you think of a time when you knew God was working in you to make you willing to obey Him? If so, describe the experience.

(b) How did God work in some Bible characters to make them willing? See, for example, Exodus 2:11—4:15; Jonah 1:1—3:3; Acts 9.

"The principle Paul lays down is this: God must work in us before He can work through us. . . . God is more interested in the workman than in the work. If the workman is what he ought to be, the work will be what it ought to be."[4]

---

10. According to verse 13, what is the ultimate goal of God's working in our lives?

Man's works are outward.
Read Philippians 2:14–18.

11. Paul then dealt with specific attitudes and actions again. How were the Philippians to work together in the church (verse 14)?

12. Look up the meaning of each of these words in a dictionary.
Murmuring

Disputing

"Were God to remove the disgruntled church members from some of our local churches, few would be left to do God's work. . . . Murmurings and disputings break our fellowship with God and with one another. Casting out these two ugly monsters is a part of the divine process for making the believer like Christ. Oh, my brethren, let us pray God to rid us of all inward discontent."[5]

13. Read 1 Corinthians 10:10. (a) To whom does this refer? (See Numbers 14:2–29.)

    (b) How did God respond to their murmuring and complaining?

    (c) Does God's view of sin ever change? Read Malachi 3:6.

14. Remembering Paul's earlier emphasis on unity (Philippians 2:1–4), we see both sins confronted here. How do people today murmur and dispute not only against God, but also against each other?

"What does it matter if external circumstances are hard? Why should they not be! If we give way to self-pity and indulge in the luxury of misery, we banish God's riches from our own lives and hinder others from entering into His provision. No sin is worse than the sin of self-pity, because it obliterates God and puts self-interest upon the throne. It opens our mouths to spit out murmurings and our lives become craving spiritual sponges, there is nothing lovely or generous about them."[6]

15. What are three descriptions of believers' lives when they obey the command not to murmur and dispute (verse 15)?

16. On the other hand, what will result from murmurings and disputings in believers' lives?

"The contrast between a Christian, who is completely blameless, and the world, completely perverted, is a study in opposites. While most Christians are far from being depraved in their life, any impurity for this reason stands out all the more. F. C. Synge aptly captions Philippians 2:14-18, 'AVOID THE FAULTS OF ISRAEL.' The history of Israel is indeed a record of failure, especially in avoiding murmurings and disputings."[7]

---

17. If our lives are blameless, harmless, and without rebuke, how will we appear in this dark, wicked world?

18. What did the Lord Jesus say would be the result of letting our light shine? Read Matthew 5:16.

19. What was Paul's motive in "holding forth the word of life" (holding firmly to the gospel; verse 16)?

20. How did Paul feel about the possibility of his blood being poured out in martyrdom for his faith and the faith of the believers (verse 17)?

21. What did Paul encourage the Philippians to do (verse 18)?

When we are not murmuring and disputing, we are able to share joy. Can you share joy?

 From My Heart

I'm learning each day that the Christian life truly is a life of faith and a process of working out our salvation. By a step of faith, I was saved; by a gradual process of God's working in me and my working out my salvation, He makes me into a vessel fit for His use and prepared for every good work (2 Timothy 2:21).

The potter and the clay is a beautiful picture of the sanctification process. The clay is put into the potter's hands, submitting itself to whatever the potter desires to do with it and make of it. It is impossible for the clay to make itself into a beautiful vessel; it is powerless to perform without the help of the potter's hand. So it is in my life. My part is to submit and trust; God's part is to fashion and mold me. If God's molding process becomes severe and hurtful, will I continue to submit and trust, or will I murmur and complain?

When I have experienced severe trials, I have sometimes felt as if I were whirling around in circles on the potter's wheel. Other times I have felt as though I were in the potter's kiln, and the heat was more than I could bear. When these times come, I pull out the poem below and read and reread it. I'd like to share a portion of it with you:

> "Wait only upon God"; my soul, be still,
> And let thy God unfold His perfect will, . . .
> For only thus can He in thee fulfill
> His heart's desire. Oh, hinder not His hand
> From fashioning the vessel He hath planned. . . .
> And He will work with hand unfettered, free,
> His high and holy purposes through thee.
> First *on* thee must the hand of power be turned,
> Till in His love's strong fire thy dross is burned,
> And thou come forth a vessel for thy Lord. . . .
> Then, my soul, wait and be still;

> Thy God shall work for thee His perfect will.
> If thou wilt take no less, *His best* shall be
> Thy portion now and through eternity.[8]

If we chafe and rebel against God's molding process, what will happen? The vessel will be marred, and the molding process will cease until we submit again. Does God discard marred and spoiled vessels in favor of those that appear perfect? No; He starts the process again and remakes us.

Aren't you glad the Heavenly Potter is patient with these vessels of clay? I sure am!

From Your Heart

Are you resisting or submitting to God's molding process in your life? Does murmuring and complaining make the situation better? What will help your situation?

Notes

1. Arp, p. 44.

2. Hannah Whitall Smith, *The Christian's Secret of a Happy Life* (Westwood, N.J.: Fleming H. Revell Co., 1952), p. 35.

3. Briscoe, p. 82.

4. Warren W. Wiersbe, *Be Joyful* (Wheaton, Ill.: Victor Books, 1974), pp. 63, 64.

5. Strauss, pp. 125, 126.

6. Oswald Chambers, *My Utmost for His Highest* (New York: Dodd, Mead & Co., 1935), p. 137.

7. John F. Walvoord, *Philippians: Triumph in Christ* (Chicago: Moody Press, 1971), p. 67.

8. Freda Hadbury; source unknown.

LESSON 7

The Joy of Friendships
PHILIPPIANS 2:19–30

"As a son with the father, he hath served with me
in the gospel" (Philippians 2:22).

Make new friends, but keep the old;
Those are silver, these are gold.
New-made friendships, like new wine,
Age will mellow and refine.
Friendships that have stood the test—
Time and change—are surely best;
Brow may wrinkle, hair grow gray;
Friendship never knows decay.
For 'mid old friends, tried and true,
Once more we reach and youth renew.
But old friends, alas! may die;
New friends must their place supply;
Cherish friendships in your breast—
New is good, but old is best;
Make new friends, but keep the old;
Those are silver, these are gold.[1]

Friends are a precious addition to our lives. The woman who has no friends is lacking one of the richest gifts in life. Cicero said over two thousand years ago, "Friendship improves happiness and abates misery, by doubling of our joy and dividing of our grief."

The apostle Paul was not only a great preacher; he was also a great friend. He brought joy to his friends' lives, and they brought joy to his life. Paul preached to the world and mixed with great masses of people, but he also had concern about individuals.

Timothy
Read Philippians 2:19–24.

In Philippians 2:19 and 20 we see three words that are

52

indicative of a friendship: "know," "comfort," "care." As you study these verses, ask yourself, "What kind of friend am I?"

1. How did Paul indicate he had a genuine interest in his friends in Philippi (verse 19)?

2. Why did Paul want to know about the Philippians?

3. Why would Paul be comforted, or encouraged, when he heard about the Philippians? Read also 3 John 4.

4. Someone once said, "When a friend is in need, don't ask, 'Is there anything I can do?' Just think of the appropriate thing and do it!" How have you helped a friend in need, or how has a friend helped you?

> After the others have come and gone,
> I'll go and visit my friend.
> I'll let her talk of the loved one she's lost,
> again and again and again.
>
> I have no money for flowers or gifts,
> and so I'll lend her my ears.
> I cannot offer her words of advice,
> and so I'll render my tears.
>
> As her friend, I'll stand beside her,
> as she starts down a long, lonely road.
> I'll avail to her the Lord of my life
> to help her carry her load.[2]

5. Why did Paul choose Timothy to make this trip to Philippi (verse 20)?

6. Timothy was a loyal friend to Paul. How can we show loyalty to our friends?

7. Paul had no one else with whom he could have close fellowship, yet he was willing to send Timothy to the Philippians. What does this say about Paul? Review Philippians 2:3 and 4.

> "Oh, the comfort, the inexpressible comfort of feeling safe with a person; having neither to weigh thoughts nor measure words, but to pour them all out, just as they are, chaff and grain together, knowing a faithful hand will take and sift them, keep what is worth keeping, and then, with the breath of kindness, blow the rest away."[3]

8. What does it mean to be like-minded, or have a kindred spirit, with someone?

9. Why did Paul and Timothy have kindred spirits (verse 22)?

10. What was the basis of the father-son relationship Paul and Timothy shared? Read 1 Timothy 1:2, 2 Timothy 1:2, and Acts 16:1–3.

11. The Philippians already had "proof" of Timothy (verse

22). How did they know him? Read Acts 16:12–40; 18:5; 19:22; 20:3–6. (Philippi was in the province of Macedonia.)

12. Why did Paul wait before he sent Timothy to Philippi (verses 23 and 24)?

Epaphroditus
Read Philippians 2:25–30.

Paul mentioned another devoted friend, Epaphroditus. Epaphroditus was from Philippi. He had been in Rome, but Paul was sending him back to Philippi, carrying this letter to the church.

13. Why had Epaphroditus been in Rome (Philippians 4:18)?

14. (a) What words in verse 25 suggest that Paul and Epaphroditus had developed a close friendship?

(b) How do these words suggest different aspects of friendship?

15. What happened to Epaphroditus while he was caring for Paul's needs (verses 26 and 27)?

16. Why was Epaphroditus' heart so heavy (verse 26)?

17. (a) Paul recognized God's purpose in sparing Epaphroditus' life (verse 27). What was it?

(b) How does this situation illustrate Psalm 103:14?

18. "More carefully" in verse 28 means "eagerly." It has to do with speed, not caution. Why was Paul eager to have Epaphroditus return to Philippi?

19. How does verse 28 illustrate the principle of Romans 12:15?

20. Paul wanted the Philippians to honor Epaphroditus ("hold in reputation," verse 29). Why were they to do this (verse 30)?

Paul's life was enriched by these two men. They brought him joy—as did the thoughts of his friends in Philippi.

21. What friends enrich your life? Thank God for these friends. Do you have an especially close friend? Pray for that friend just now.

"A comforter-friend . . . comes alongside and offers himself as a companion in the pain or distress. Not a sermon. Not a cliché. Not an analysis. Not even an I-told-you-so. Just himself."[4]

Friendship Dos and Don'ts from Proverbs

A Friend Doesn't Do This

- 17:9—Does not break a confidence.
- 16:29—Does not entice or manipulate you into things against your better judgment.
- 3:27—Is not selfish.
- 19:6—Does not try to buy friendship or attach herself to you because of what you have or who you are.

A Friend Does Do This

- 18:24—Is available when you need her.
- 27:5, 6—Is honest when she knows you need to be rebuked.
- 19:11—Overlooks small things and does not get angry.
- 12:25—Builds up and encourages you.

22. Who is the best Friend anyone could ever have? Read John 15:13–15 and Hebrews 13:5 and 6.

 From My Heart

How well do you know me? Some of you know me as an acquaintance, some as a friend, and a few as a confidante or close friend. How well we know each other depends upon how much time we spend together. It takes time to get to know a person, to build a friendship.

How well do you know God? Is He an acquaintance, someone you speak to and read about occasionally? Is He a friend, someone you enjoy talking to and spending time with? Is He a confidante, someone you consider your closest friend, the only person who really understands everything about you and really cares about your struggles? How well you know God depends on how much time you spend together each day. A relationship that develops into a friendship takes time and work. How much time and effort are we willing to invest in developing friendship with God?

From Your Heart

Do you have a hard time making or keeping friends?
What could you do to develop a friendship with another
Christian woman? What do you need to do to develop your
friendship with God?

Notes

1. Joseph Parry, quoted by Charles L. Wallis, ed., *The Treasure Chest* (New York: Harper & Row, Publishers, 1965), p. 100.

2. J. P. Lockhart, quoted in *Mature Living* (May 1990), p. 19.

3. George Eliot, quoted by Eleanor L. Doan, compiler, *The Speaker's Sourcebook* (Grand Rapids: Zondervan Publishing House, 1960), p. 107.

4. McDonald, p. 191.

Religion or Relationship?
PHILIPPIANS 3:1–11

---

*"That I may know him, and the power of his resurrection,
and the fellowship of his sufferings, being made conformable
unto his death" (Philippians 3:10).*

We see the theme of the book of Philippians occurring again as Paul continued his letter to his brothers and sisters in Christ at Philippi. "Rejoice in the Lord in spite of your circumstances" is Paul's continuing message. He had dealt with various problems that could rob the Philippians of their joy. Now he attacked another problem that interfered with the joy of the church at Philippi.

The problem was not something happening to him or to them; the problem was false teachers. No one could speak better on this subject than Paul because he had once been one of these false teachers. False teachers and false religion can rob us of joy.

False religion: confidence in the flesh
Read Philippians 3:1–3.

1. Why did Paul remind the Philippians to rejoice in the Lord (verse 1) as he began to expose those who desired to turn them away from the Lord?

"Having an almighty and most loving Father, in whom we live, and move, and have our being, let us rejoice in Him. Having a most loving Saviour, who has made Himself our brother, and feeds us with His life, we ought surely to rejoice in Him. Having the Holy Spirit of God with us, making us

59

His temples, and pouring His love into our hearts,
we ought certainly to answer His love, and re-
joice in His overflowing goodness. 'Rejoice in the
Lord.' . . ."[1]

2. Paul acknowledged that he had already taught the Philippians about false teachers. (a) Why did he bring up the
subject again?

(b) Of what lessons do you need to be continually reminded? How can you keep those lessons fresh in
your mind?

Here are some terms you need to know in order to fully
understand this lesson: **Judaizers**—Those who taught that
Christians must be circumcised and follow the law of Moses
in order to have a relationship with God (Acts 15:1). These
pharisaical Judaizers had added hundreds of traditions to
the law. They had altered the law of Moses into 365 negative
commandments and 205 positive commandments. The keeping of these laws made a man righteous according to their
teachings.

Circumcision—The rite of circumcision was instituted
by God in Genesis 17 to seal the covenant made to Abraham.
It was required before the law of Moses was given in Exodus
20. Circumcision was an outward sign of a man's faith in God
and in the promises of God.

Legalism—Legalism is relying on one's own resources
to meet God's standards; it is trying to keep all the rules to
please God. Pride or confidence in the flesh can easily take
over if a person feels he is keeping more rules than someone
else.

Paul labeled these false teachers as dogs (verse 2).
They were behaving like dogs, tearing and destroying with
this kind of teaching. He also called them evil workers (causing schisms and divisions) and the concision. Circumcision
was honorable in God's sight, but Paul would not even use
the word in connection with these false teachers. He called

it "concision," which means "mutilation." The Judaizers were still teaching the need for a fleshy circumcision.

3. What did Paul say about circumcision in Romans 2:27–29?

4. Why do you think Paul repeated the word "beware" three times?

5. How do you think false teaching could affect a believer's life? How could it rob a believer of joy? If you have been involved in false teaching, relate how it affected your life.

Old Testament—Under Law	New Testament—Under Grace
Fleshly circumcision	Heart circumcision
Genesis 17	Romans 2:27–29
• Physical	• Spiritual
• Outward	• Inward
• Rite	• Reality

6. How did Paul describe true circumcision, or a true Christian (verse 3)?

7. How do people put confidence in the flesh?

8. How do we know we cannot earn or gain Heaven by things we do in the flesh? Read Isaiah 64:6, Ephesians 2:8 and 9, and Titus 3:5 and 6.

"If my good works had put me into Christ, then my bad works might turn me out of him. But since he put me in when I was a sinner, vile and worthless, he will never take me out, though I am a sinner vile and worthless still."[2]

Relationship: confidence in Christ
Read Philippians 3:4–11.

Having warned the Philippians against legalism that demands outward performance, Paul then gave his testimony concerning his deliverance from confidence in the flesh.

The Judaizers emphasized the externals—circumcision and keeping the commandments. If anyone wanted to boast of externals and achievements, unconverted Paul was the one who could do it (verse 4). If there had been magazines in Paul's day, his picture would have been on several covers as "Man of the Year." As Saul of Tarsus, he was famous and influential, proud of his zeal for God.

9. Read verses 5 and 6 and record the things about which Paul could boast.

   Pride of race

   Pride of family

   Pride of religion

   Pride of zeal

   Pride of morality

10. Paul had much in which to boast. But what was his appraisal of his past achievements and religious heritage (verse 7)?

"Great losses create a condition in which Christ can become real to us—the condition of helplessness. It brought Paul to salvation. He was on the road to Damascus when he was struck broadside

by God. Deprived of sight, he saw for the first time that what he had banked on for his salvation—lawkeeping, zeal, heritage—was worthless. But in the wake of his loss came a personal knowledge of Jesus as Savior and Lord. And it was out of this continuing sense of helplessness that it grew deeper. Have you had a devastating loss? If you are not a Christian, let this experience lead you to see your need to receive Jesus as your Savior. And if you are a child of God, let Him pick up the pieces and build something new and better."[3]

11. What did it cost you when you established a personal relationship with Jesus Christ?

12. Read verse 8. How did Paul feel about his losses?

". . . We are reminded of Jim Eliot's [sic] words: 'He is no fool to give what he cannot keep to gain what he cannot lose.' This is what Paul experienced: he lost his religion and his reputation, but he gained far more than he lost."[4]

13. Read verse 9. Paul no longer counted on being saved by keeping the law. What did he depend upon for his salvation?

14. When he was converted, Paul received "the righteousness which is of God by faith." Read the following verses and note how God's righteousness becomes ours.

    Romans 3:12; 4:5

1 Corinthians 1:30

2 Corinthians 5:21

"True righteousness comes from God through faith in Christ. It is God's gift. He is the source of righteousness. Christ is the procuror, and faith is the channel. As water comes to us from a source and through a channel, righteousness comes from God to sinners through the channel of their faith in Christ. Adorning sinners in the righteousness of Christ is an act of God; it is not an accomplishment of man."[5]

Since living for Christ was the driving force of Paul's life (Philippians 1:21), Paul wanted to know Christ more fully (verse 10).

15. (a) How do we really get to know a person?

(b) How can we know Christ and build an intimate relationship with Him? Read John 5:39.

I once heard a missionary speak on Philippians 3:10: "that I may know Him." She was sharing how she wanted to know Christ in a more intimate way. She went on to say that the longer people live together, the better they get to know each other—they even begin to look alike. Then she said, "Maybe that's why I'm not married; no one wants to look like me."

16. What two things about Christ did Paul particularly want to know (verse 10)?

17. Read Paul's prayer in Ephesians 1:15–21. How will our lives be different if we experience Christ's power?

18. How can we have this power in our lives? Read Romans 6:8–12 and Galatians 5:16 and 17.

We all want power in our lives, but who wants suffering? No one really wants it; but if we grow in our knowledge of Christ and begin to experience His power in our lives, suffering will come. We need to get ready for it and expect it. (This is the kind of suffering Paul referred to earlier, Philippians 1:29.)

19. Read 1 Peter 4:13. How should we respond to such suffering?

"The order of the verse [Philippians 3:10] (living Savior, resurrection, death) reflects the experience of the believer, whereas it was just the opposite in the historical occurrence. Christ suffered before He was raised, but a believer will suffer if he manifests resurrection power in his daily living."[6]

---

20. Do you back away from getting to know Christ when you realize suffering will be involved? Read 1 Peter 2:21–23 and Hebrews 4:15 and 16. What help is available to you?

Paul wanted to experience Christ's resurrection power and the fellowship of His sufferings, but he looked beyond these things to the future resurrection (verse 11). Paul was not doubting the resurrection of his body ("if by any means"). He was expressing uncertainty regarding whether or not he would be resurrected as a martyr.

"Christians have no tidy answers to suffering, no easy ten principles for happy sufferers. They only have attitudes for meeting it, handles for overcoming it, outlooks for transcending it."[7]

---

21. If we want what Paul had—resurrection power and the right attitude toward suffering—what must we also do? Read 1 Corinthians 15:31.

". . . When we look at Scripture, we find no room for a painless commitment. There is no resurrection without a crucifixion. No cross, no empty tomb. It takes a cross to fill the tomb in order to give resurrection a chance to empty it."[8]

Paul didn't want to be just an ordinary Christian. He wanted to attain a lifestyle that was different, supernatural. He wanted to appear as alive from the dead—a living person walking among dead people.

22. How are you different from the spiritually dead people around you?

 From My Heart

Many people today are changing churches or religions. Paul didn't change religions—he was converted to Christ. He was radically and thoroughly changed when He met His Lord and Master, Jesus Christ, on the Damascus Road.

When I was cleaning out some of my husband's files, I found the following poem. I do not know if a man or a woman wrote the poem, but I do know one thing about the author: he or she was radically transformed by a personal relationship with Jesus Christ—just as Paul was.

> I had walked life's way with an easy tread,
> Had followed where comfort and pleasures led,
> Until one day in a quiet place
> I met the Master face to face.
>
> With station and rank and wealth for my goal,
> Much thought for my body but none for my soul,
> I had entered to win in life's mad race,
> When I met the Master face to face.

I met Him and knew Him and blushed to see
That His eyes full of sorrow were fixed on me;
And I faltered and fell at His feet that day
While my castles melted and vanished away.

Melted and vanished, and in their place,
Naught else did I see but the Master's face;
And I cried aloud, "Oh, make me meet
To follow the steps of Thy wounded feet."

My thought is now for the souls of men;
I have lost my life to find it again,
E'er since one day in a quiet place
I met the Master face to face.

From Your Heart

Have you ever met the Master face to face? Are you depending on religion to get you to Heaven or a relationship with Jesus Christ? Why not settle this matter today and start developing a close relationship with Him.

Notes

1. William Bernard Ullathorne, quoted by Tileston, p. 146.

2. Spurgeon, quoted by Carter, p. 185.

3. "Life's Losses," *Our Daily Bread* (Grand Rapids: Radio Bible Class, December—February 1993), February 4.

4. Wiersbe, p. 88.

5. Arp, p. 60.

6. Robert G. Gromacki, *Stand United in Joy: An Exposition of Philippians* (Grand Rapids: Baker Book House, 1980), p. 152.

7. Paul Malte, quoted by Joel A. Freeman, *"God Is Not Fair": Coming to Terms with Life's Raw Deals* (San Bernardino, Calif.: Here's Life Publishers, 1987), p. 20.

8. Briscoe, pp. 117, 118.

LESSON 9

Winners Never Quit

PHILIPPIANS 3:12-15

"I press toward the mark for the prize of the high calling of God in Christ Jesus" (Philippians 3:14).

Paul wanted to know Christ so well that resurrection power would characterize his life. The more Paul knew Christ, the more he would be like Christ. Paul knew that he had not yet attained that goal, even though he had been converted to Christ almost thirty years before he wrote to the Philippians. However, he kept striving.

How can today's Christian women ever attain that kind of lifestyle? The same way Paul did! Christlikeness must be our daily goal. We will not attain Christlikeness overnight; it is a lifelong process.

Paul gave three directives that will help us as we reach for the goal of Christlikeness: (1) examine yourself; (2) don't look back; (3) keep your eye on the goal.

In Philippians 3:12–15 Paul used five words or phrases that illustrate a person in a race: "attain," "follow after," "apprehend," "reaching forth," and "press toward." Paul pictured himself as one running in a race, giving everything he had to win the race and receive the prize.

Examine yourself.
Read Philippians 3:12.

Saul of Tarsus—the person Paul described in Philippians 3:4–6—was a proud man. But that changed when Saul—now Paul—was converted.

1. How did Paul display humility? What had he not yet attained? Review verse 10.

2. The verb "perfect" in verse 12 is in the perfect tense in the Greek language. That means the action was completed in the past but the results continue in the present. Paul said he was not perfected once for all when he was saved. Read Romans 7:18–21. What does this passage teach about sin in the Christian life?

The Judaizers, whom Paul warned about in verse 2, may have claimed sinless perfection. But Paul reminded the Philippians that this was not possible even though it was his goal.

3. Paul said he followed after or overextended himself to apprehend, or capture, that for which Christ captured him. What purpose did God have in mind for Paul when He captured him? Read Galatians 1:15 and 16.

4. What is God's purpose for us? Read Romans 8:29.

"Everything in life may help us to be more like the Lord Jesus. The routine work of every day, the periods of reading and studying, the moments spent in rest and relaxation, the trials and suffering that may come to us, all must be used to achieve the goal of Christlikeness. When this 'one thing' is always before us we will not respond unfavorably, no matter the nature of the circumstance that comes to us. All must contribute to conform us unto the image of Him whose we are and whom we serve. To this we are divinely chosen by God."[1]

Paul never forgot why Christ had captured him on the road to Damascus. Paul began the race toward Christlikeness that day.

5. How are you doing in the Christian race? Take a few minutes to examine yourself. Picture yourself in a race. Are you sitting on the bench? warming up? at the starting line? huffing and puffing in the race?

If you are sitting on the bench, get up and get started again. Remember, we don't stand still in the Christian life; we are going either forward or backward.

> *"What assists us in keeping eternal value in clear view? What keeps us joyfully advancing when every bone and tissue in our body is yelling, 'Quit! Throw in the towel'?... The cross of Jesus Christ."[2]*

Don't look back.
Read Philippians 3:13.

6. What does "I count not myself to have apprehended" mean?

7. Staying in the race of life takes a lot of concentration. Paul indicated he did "one thing" to keep himself in the race. What was it?

> *"What he [Paul] had already accomplished would not help him reach his goal in the future. He did not lose all memory of the past, but he refused to let the past impede his progress."[3]*

8. What do Hebrews 12:1 and 2 say our focus should be?

9. If you had to express a singular purpose for your life, what would it be?

10. Why do we need to forget our past failures if we want to run well?

"About those regrets. Surely you know they are forgiven? It would be wiser now, if you think of them at all, to see them as stepping stones toward knowledge. It is a waste to think of them in any other way, for I turn all regrets into resources. Have you thought of this? To emphasize your failures is actually to de-emphasize My power! . . . Will you choose to trust Me? Remember, trusting, like any other action, is a choice. And while you are making choices, why don't you also decide to make this one—choose to forgive yourself! Self-inflicted punishment can do nothing to alter the past, and continuing remorse is of no value at all. Forgiveness means you are free from your yesterdays—forever!"[4]

11. We can never totally forget our past, so how can we move on? Read Psalm 103:12, Hebrews 10:17, and 1 John 1:9.

We must forget even past accomplishments and blessings. Paul had established churches from Jerusalem to Spain; he could have said, "I've done enough." He could have looked at all the suffering he had endured and concluded, "I've suffered enough," but he didn't. Paul didn't view his life as a relay race; he knew he wasn't going to pass the baton to someone else. Paul viewed his life as a constant race until he saw Christ. Only then would the goal be reached and the race be over.

12. What did the Lord Jesus say about a person who looks back? Read Luke 9:62.

"We love to pull out our scrapbooks and read the clippings. We love to luxuriate in the achievements of the past. Granted, we should be able to indulge ourselves in a few whimsical moments,

reminiscing. But watch out! Sad is the individual who has only the clippings of the past. . . . Live with your back to the past."⁵

13. The writer of Hebrews also pictured the Christian life as a race in 12:1. What do Hebrews 12:1 and Philippians 3:13 teach us about how we should run the race?

14. Complete the following chart:

Forget Them	Go for Them
Things that are hindering your spiritual growth	Things you are aiming for in your spiritual life

Keep your eye on the goal.
Read Philippians 3:14 and 15.

"Past laps do not matter in a race; the laps that stretch ahead are the ones that matter. The goal lies at the completion of all the laps. Paul knew this. He understood that what he had accomplished was past; he focused on the future."⁶

15. What words in verse 14 picture the endurance it takes to stay in a race?

16. (a) What was the prize for which Paul was striving?

    (b) What kind of prize was it? Read 1 Corinthians 9:25.

> *"In verse 14 the apostle is not speaking of the prize that God gives the believer as the victor and overcomer in the race. Other passages of Scripture teach that. Paul says, 'For me there is a prize in the high calling that God gave us in Christ. It is to be like him.' "[7]*

17. Read 1 Corinthians 9:24–27. How did Paul describe the way he ran the race?

18. What will help us when we feel like dropping out of the race? Read Hebrews 12:1–3.

19. When Paul wrote his second letter to Timothy, Paul knew his martyrdom was imminent. What was his final testimony in 2 Timothy 4:7?

20. We must keep pressing on until we reach the goal. When will this take place? Read 1 John 3:2.

The word "perfect" in verse 15, an adjective, is a different word than the "perfect" in verse 12, a verb. In verse 15 "perfect" means "to be mature, becoming full grown."

21. What is Paul's challenge to mature believers?

> *"It is possible to be a well-instructed fundamentalist who has progressed in Bible study, attended a lot of meetings, and learned 'all the answers,' and yet not be much like Jesus. . . . A mature Christian is one who has grown in Bible Christlikeness, not merely graduated in Bible courses."[8]*

From My Heart

Yes, the Christian life is like a race, but there is one big difference between the race of life and a track race. In the Christian life we can all be winners if we don't give up before we finish the race.

I once heard that the most famous speech Winston Churchill ever made consisted of twelve words and lasted two minutes. This was the message: "Never give up. Never, never give up. Never, never, never give up." Will we, like Paul, be able to say as we near the finish line, "I have finished my course, I have kept the faith" (2 Timothy 4:7)?

My husband and I often shared with our boys in their formative years this famous saying, "Quitters never win, and winners never quit." Those words still ring in my mind when I'm tempted to slow down in the race and start thinking about how comfortable it would be to just sit on the bench for a while. However, I want to be a winner and finish the race. How about you?

From Your Heart

Where are you in life's race? (Review your answer to question 5.) What do you need to do to get moving toward the goal?

Notes

1. Strauss, p. 184.
2. Freeman, p. 87.
3. Arp, p. 66.
4. Charles Slagle, *From the Father's Heart* (Shippensburg, Pa.: Destiny Image Publishers), p. 112.
5. Huffman, p. 64.
6. Arp, p. 67.
7. J. Dwight Pentecost, *The Joy of Living: A Study of Philippians* (Grand Rapids: The Zondervan Corporation, 1973), p. 151.
8. Vance Havner, *Day by Day* (Old Tappan, N.J.: Fleming H. Revell Co., 1958), p. 241.

LESSON 10

Do You Walk What You Talk?

PHILIPPIANS 3:16–21

"Brethren, be followers together of me, and mark them which walk so as ye have us for an ensample" (Philippians 3:17).

Chapter 3 started with a warning about false teachers, namely the Judaizers. Then Paul explained what a true Christian is (verse 3) and the importance of a Christlike life (verses 4–15). Then Paul exhorted the Philippians to walk the same walk and have the same mind about what a true Christian is. Paul warned them about a group of people he describes as "enemies of the cross of Christ: whose end is destruction, whose God is their belly . . . who mind earthly things" (verses 18 and 19).

Paul was saying, "These people will lead you astray." Whom should the Philippians follow? Those who were modeling Christlikeness. The same message is good for us today.

The Christian walk
Read Philippians 3:16 and 17.

1. (a) What had the Philippians already attained? Read Philippians 1:1.

   (b) What did Paul exhort them to do in Philippians 3:16?

2. In verse 17 Paul told the believers to follow his example. In what way did he want them to follow him? Read 1 Corinthians 11:1 and Philippians 1:21.

75

> *"John Newton [author of the song 'Amazing Grace']*
> *is reported to have said: 'I have ever to confess,*
> *with sorrow, that I am far from being what I ought*
> *to be, and far from what I wish to be, but also—*
> *blessed be God's name!—to testify that I am far,*
> *very far, from what I once was.' . . . Every man,*
> *without thought or intention or consciousness of*
> *it, is ever an example that someone else will*
> *follow."[1]*

3. Paul did not stand alone as an excellent example to follow. He said, "Mark them." To whom may he have referred? Read Philippians 2:19, 20, 25, and 26.

4. Whom have you read about or whom do you know who is an example of godliness to you? What spiritual qualities does this person have?

5. Why is it important for us to have contemporary models of godliness?

6. Each of us is a model—whether intentionally or not. Who is watching us? Review Philippians 2:15, and read Matthew 5:13–16.

> *"How often have you hid behind your humanity?*
> *How often have you said to yourself, 'Well, I'm a*
> *sinner saved by grace. I'm not perfect. I'm not*
> *expected to be!' You may use that as a rationaliza-*
> *tion to avoid being the person Christ wants you to*
> *be. You are either a good example or a bad*
> *example of Christianity."[2]*

The worldly walk
Read Philippians 3:18 and 19.

Paul lived the life he lived because he saw the error of Judaism and was saved from the dead works of that system. He described another group of people whom we would call liberals. The chart below shows the difference between the legalist and the liberal. Paul did not denounce these people with a smug gloating, but with an aching heart.

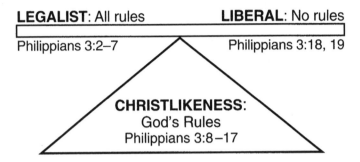

LEGALIST: All rules   **LIBERAL**: No rules

Philippians 3:2–7   Philippians 3:18, 19

CHRISTLIKENESS:
God's Rules
Philippians 3:8–17

7. Paul gave us a glimpse of his heart as he wrote so severely about those who profess Christ but do not follow Him. How did he feel (verse 18)?

8. How do we know these "enemies of the cross" were professors of salvation but not possessors? Read verse 19. Read also 2 Thessalonians 1:8–10 and Matthew 7:13.

9. The church has always had to be on guard against false teachers. How do the enemies of the cross sometimes appear? Read 2 Corinthians 11:13–15.

10. Read 2 Timothy 4:3 and 4 and 2 Peter 2:1–3. What can we expect as the coming of Christ draws nearer?

11. What false teachers or teachings are prevalent in our day?

12. How should you feel about a friend or relative who has been deceived by a false teacher?

13. Paul gave four characteristics of these false teachers in verse 19. What are they?

14. What does "whose God is their belly" mean? Read also Romans 16:18.

"Chasing after pleasure is a confession of an unsatisfied life."[3]

---

15. If a woman's mind is set only on earthly things, what will she be living for? Read Luke 12:19 and 1 Corinthians 15:32.

16. In contrast to this mind-set, what should be true of the believer? Read Colossians 3:1–3.

17. What things in life are really important to you? How many of them have eternal value?

We all need to review often the following words in order to keep eternal values foremost in our minds: "Only one life—twill soon be passed. Only what's done for Christ will last."

Our last walk
Read Philippians 3:20 and 21.

The enemies of the cross built castles on earth, but Paul reminded his readers that God is preparing a heavenly Home for His own. This is cause for rejoicing!

18. What does the word "conversation" mean in verse 20? Review the use of this same word in Philippians 1:27 (lesson 4, p. 31).

19. How do Ephesians 2:19 and 1 Peter 2:11 prove that our citizenship is in Heaven?

"Christians . . . constitute a colony of heaven on earth. They have double citizenship. Paul was in the kingdom of God, and yet he claimed and used the rights of his Roman citizenship. . . ."[4]

---

20. When do we expect the Savior to return and take us to Heaven? Read Titus 2:13 and 1 Thessalonians 4:13–16.

21. Our present bodies are not conditioned for our heavenly state. They are lowly bodies (the literal meaning of "vile"), subject to disease and death. How is God going to fit us for Heaven? Read verse 21 and 1 Corinthians 15:50–54.

22. What will our glorified bodies be like? Read John 20:17–20, 26 and 1 John 3:2.

23. Christ will "subdue all things unto himself" (verse 21). What will this involve? Read 1 Corinthians 15:24–28.

24. Resurrected believers will spend eternity in Heaven with God. What will happen to resurrected unbelievers? Read Revelation 20:11–15.

"When I get to heaven, I shall see three wonders there—the first wonder will be to see many people there whom I did not expect to see; the second wonder will be to miss many people whom I did expect to see; and the third and greatest wonder of all will be to find myself there."[5]

God's plan of salvation is so simple, but I fear many will stumble over the cross of Christ into an eternal Hell, thinking they were going to Heaven. If you are still not positive Heaven will be your eternal Home, please review the last part of lesson 1 again.

 ## *From My Heart*

Have you read Matthew 7:13 and 14 lately? It is heart-wrenching to realize only a few people are walking the narrow way that leads to eternal life. Many are on the broad road to eternal destruction. Why are so few people being saved? Could it be because so few Christians walk what they talk?

Maybe we are too earthly minded. Maybe we have gotten too comfortable down here, living as if this were our final home. How many of us are really living like foreigners and strangers, waiting for Heaven? I fear I seldom live like that. I need to keep my heart and affections set on heavenly things. If I started each day with the firm expectation that Christ could return that day, I'm sure I would be more heavenly minded.

The following story was a rebuke to me. Six-year-old Sally heard the pastor preaching about Heaven and the Rapture. When she got home, she asked her mother if Christ could really come at any time. Her mother said yes. Sally asked, "Could He come today?" Mother said yes. "Mommy, would you comb my hair?" asked Sally.

Would you change anything about your life if you knew Jesus Christ would return today?

From Your Heart

Do your friends and relatives know you are a Christian? Does your Christian walk and talk bring honor to Christ? In what areas do you need to make changes?

Notes
1. Strauss, pp. 198, 199.
2. Huffman, p. 73.
3. Benjamin R. De Jong, *Uncle Ben's Quotebook* (Irvine, Calif.: Harvest House Publishers, 1976), p. 301.
4. Gromacki, p. 167.
5. John Newton, quoted by John Blanchard, compiler, *Gathered Gold* (Durham, England: Evangelical Press, 1984), p. 139.

LESSON 11
A Sure Cure for Worry
PHILIPPIANS 4:1-9

"Be careful for nothing; but in every thing by prayer and supplication with thanksgiving let your requests be made known unto God" (Philippians 4:6).

Philippians 4:1–9 gives us a sure cure for worry. Is there anyone who doesn't need it? I sure do! For many of us, worry is our Number One joy-killer.

We all know worrying is ridiculous, yet we still do it. Worry is futile and a waste of time. Worry is concern about something we can usually do nothing about, something that may not even happen or something that has happened and can't be changed. One person made this comment about worry, "Worry about yesterday or tomorrow saps us of the strength we need to do today's work."

Paul gave four directives to help us out of the vicious, useless cycle of worry: (1) rejoice; (2) pray; (3) think correctly; (4) obey.

Sounds so simple—and it is! The question is, Will we use the prescription? If I go to the doctor and he gives me a prescription to heal my illness and I don't take the prescription, I'm asking for serious problems. If God gives me a prescription to heal my worries and I won't use it, I'm asking for serious problems as well. The choice is mine. No one can do it for me because worry is an "inside job." Only the Lord and I can solve this problem.

Rejoice.
Read Philippians 4:1–5.

Before Paul approached the problem that was causing strife and worry in the Philippian church, he told the believers to "stand fast in the Lord."

82

1. (a) What does standing fast, or firm, in the Lord mean?

   (b) Why do you think Paul told the Philippians this a second time? (The first time is in 1:27.)

2. (a) What phrase is repeated in verses 1, 2, and 4?

   (b) What does each of those verses say about the Lord?

3. Two ladies in the Philippian church, Euodias and Syntyche, were having a disagreement that was threatening the unity of the church (verse 2). What did Paul urge, or implore ("beseech"), the women to do?

4. How do women act toward one another when they are not like-minded?

"Since men and women have distinctive personalities, there are bound to be differences of opinion. People have various tastes in food, clothes, and hobbies. In spiritual matters, however, there should be unity. . . . Refusal to do so [be like-minded] indicates a spirit of carnality and disobedience."[1]

---

5. Paul evidently knew these women would respond to counsel, so he asked a fellow servant to help them. What positive thing did Paul note about these women (verse 3)?

Having dealt with the problem in the church, Paul returned to this theme: rejoice in the Lord (verse 4). Paul exhorted the Philippians to be always full of joy in the Lord, no matter what was going on in their lives.

This joy is ESSENTIAL—God commands it!

This joy is SUPERNATURAL—Only those in the Lord can obey this command.

This joy is PERPETUAL—Always rejoice.

"Joy as used in Philippians is a cheerfulness that comes from being calm. With God at the controls of your life, you can be calm no matter what you feel like."[2]

---

6. "Constant rejoicing should be an integral part of the believer's inner response to life's pleasant *and* difficult situations."[3] How can we have joy regardless of the circumstances? Read the following verses and note the things in which we can always rejoice.

Romans 5:2

Romans 15:13

1 Thessalonians 2:19, 20

1 Peter 1:8

"To rejoice in the Lord does not mean to ignore your responsibilities, neither does it mean to evade obvious issues. Rather, it means to be fully cognizant of the situation, fully prepared to deal

> *with it responsibly, and fully convinced of the power of the Lord to give you wisdom, grace and courage to deal with whatever comes along. When this attitude is adopted it will not produce a giddy irresponsibility or a naive ecstasy, but a deep, mature, responsible faith that has as its core a majestic Lord. When He is the One at the core, joy can result because of the certainty of His ultimate triumph, the assurance of His benevolent purpose and the opportunities for spiritual growth that the situation affords."[4]*

7. How will the joy of the Lord affect us? Read Nehemiah 8:10.

> *"If you have the whine in you, kick it out ruthlessly. It is a positive crime to be weak in God's strength."[5]*

8. Look up the word "moderation" (verse 5) in a different translation or a Bible dictionary. What does it mean?

9. Give some everyday situations where we find it difficult to show an unselfish and considerate disposition.

10. What should motivate us to gentleness? Read 2 Thessalonians 2:2, Hebrews 10:37, and James 5:8.

11. If we expect Christ to return at any moment, how will this affect our lives? Read 1 John 2:28.

Pray.
Read Philippians 4:6 and 7.

"Be careful" in verse 6 can be translated "Don't be anxious." We would say, "Don't worry." Worry is anxious care that does not trust God and thus is sin.

12. What specific things does the Bible command us not to worry about? Read Matthew 6:25 and 34.

"When we focus upon tomorrow, the chemical and electrical energies of the body are frustrated, because they are poured into the body, but not used. They cannot be released in action, because we cannot act upon the future. Rather than releasing bodily energy through productive activity, worry activates more and more energy that is unused, some of which in chemical form may eat away at the lining of the stomach. All of your time and your energy and your efforts ought to be burned up during today which God has given to you, not transformed into worry about tomorrow which belongs to Him."[6]

---

13. Worry begins when we fear we are inadequate for a situation. What does the Bible say about our adequacy? Read Matthew 6:27 and 2 Corinthians 3:5.

14. What does the Bible say about God's ability? Read Matthew 6:30 and 2 Corinthians 3:5.

15. When we admit our inadequacy and God's ability, we can let go of worry. According to verse 6, what are we to do in place of worrying?

Note three steps in making our requests known to God.

• By prayer or adoration—Before we make our requests known, we must worship and adore God in prayer, acknowledging His greatness and power to do the impossible.

• By supplication—Bring our needs to Him. Ask Him!

• With thanksgiving—We need to develop an attitude of gratitude for what God is allowing in our lives rather than worrying about what is happening.

> I prayed for relief from my burden,
> Asked the Lord to take it away,
> But I grew unsettled and doubtful,
> For the burden grew harder each day;
> Then I changed the note of my praying,
> And asked for the Master alone,
> Then turned to take up my burden—
> But lo! my burden was gone.
>
> So now, if I'm burdened or doubtful,
> Or weary with overmuch care,
> I go at once to my Saviour,
> Ask Him the burden to share;
> And I find Him ever so willing,
> For He walks by my side, on the road,
> Now, wonder of wonders, I'm telling,
> He takes from my heart all the load![7]

16. God never promises us that our problems will go away, but what does He promise to do? Read Psalm 55:22.

17. What comes into our hearts and minds in place of worry (verse 7)?

18. What will the peace of God do for us?

> Oh, for the peace of perfect trust,
> My loving God, in Thee;
> Unwavering faith, that never doubts,
> Thou chooseth best for me.
>
> That hears Thy voice—a Father's voice—
> Directing for the best.
> Oh, for the peace of a perfect trust,
> A heart for Thee at rest.[8]

Think correctly.
Read Philippians 4:8.

Paul gave another part of the antidote for worry in verse 8: think correctly. "A believer must daily strengthen the moral integrity of his thought life. Solomon observed: 'For as he thinketh in his heart, so is he' (Prov. 23:7)."[9]

19. Explain how each of these characteristics of correct thinking will promote peace and joy and will defeat worry in our lives.

Think about things that are *true* (morally upright, dependable).

Think about things that are *honest* (noble, honorable).

Think about things that are *just* (right).

Think about things that are *pure* (morally pure).

Think about things that are *lovely* (pleasing, agreeable).

Think about things that are of *good report* (praiseworthy, constructive).

When our minds are filled with these kinds of thoughts, our thought life will be virtuous and worthy of praise.

20. (a) What causes our minds to be filled with negative, worrisome thoughts?

(b) On what should we meditate to have positive, wholesome thoughts? Read Psalm 119:165.

Obey.
Read Philippians 4:9.

21. We must do one more thing to enjoy God's peace. What is it? Read John 13:17.

"The golden summary of our life is to be this: as to the past, a record of gratitude; as to the present, a record of service; and as to the future, a record of trust."[10]

 From My Heart
_____

Worry destroys, saddens, and kills. It saps our energy and causes physical problems. It cripples our spiritual nature and causes us to feel poor and helpless. Worry is a very destructive pasttime, yet we continue to do it.

Most of us would never consider destroying our minds and bodies with alcohol or drugs, but somehow we look at worry as a legitimate sin. We excuse ourselves by saying, "I know I shouldn't do it, but I just can't stop."

We can no longer use that excuse after studying this lesson. We now have a sure cure, and it could be summarized in three words: Pray about everything. Yes, we must turn every care into a prayer. Transfer the worrisome, negative thoughts into powerful, positive prayers, and God promises that you will have peace.

If all Christians were asked to form two lines, the Worry

Warts and the Prayer Warriors, in which line would you belong? Would you want to be standing in that line when Christ returns?

From Your Heart

What one thing do you worry about the most? What does God want you to do with this worry? When are you going to begin to obey God?

Notes

  1. Gromacki, p. 174.
  2. Cheryl Fawcett, "He Brings Me Joy," *Cedarville Torch* (Spring 1993), p. 11.
  3. Gromacki, p. 176.
  4. Briscoe, pp. 135, 136.
  5. Chambers, p. 105.
  6. Jay E. Adams, *What to Do about Worry* (Nutley, N.J.: Presbyterian and Reformed Publishing Co., 1975), p. 7.
  7. Agnes K. King, quoted by Al Bryant, compiler, *Climbing the Heights* (Grand Rapids: Zondervan Publishing House, 1956), December 5.
  8. Quoted by Bryant, April 30.
  9. Gromacki, p. 183.
  10. D. M. Panton, quoted by Mrs. Charles E. Cowman, *Streams in the Desert—2* (Grand Rapids: Zondervan Publishing House, 1966), pp. 368, 369.

Contentment in Spite of Circumstances

PHILIPPIANS 4:11–23

---

*"I have learned, in whatsoever state I am,
therewith to be content" (Philippians 4:11).*

Philippians 4:6–8 deals with living without worry and having a life of peace and joy. It seems natural that a person whose life was filled with prayer and praise would be content. Yet learning to be content with poverty or plenty may not have been an easy lesson for Paul to learn, considering his background. Remember, affluence had been his way of life before he came to know the Savior.

Paul had been brought up as a Roman citizen. Nothing could be more humiliating for such a man than to be imprisoned. How did he manage? Paul said he had learned to be content in every situation he faced in life. How? Paul shared an extraordinary concept: real freedom comes from turning loose of everything. He had found greater contentment in being without and going hungry but with Christ at the center of his life than he had ever found having plenty and feasting as a wealthy man. Sounds like "palms-up living": "Lord, give what You want, or take what You want."

We also can learn to live this contented life. Let's find out how.

The sovereignty of God
Read Philippians 4:10–12.

God is sovereign. He does what He chooses, how He chooses, when He chooses in our lives. Paul saw God's sovereign plan arranging circumstances and situations for the fulfilling of the Father's purpose in his life. He didn't resent

91

God's plan; he just learned to adjust to it and even learned to be content with it. Accepting the sovereignty of God is a great source of contentment.

One adjustment Paul had learned to make regarded financial support. The Philippians had taken it upon themselves to partially support Paul when he left their town. After some time, the support stopped. Some Bible scholars feel Paul hadn't heard from the Philippians for as long as ten years and he didn't know why. That is why he was so overjoyed in having heard from them now.

1. Did Paul expect or demand support from the churches? Read 2 Corinthians 11:9 and 1 Thessalonians 2:9.

2. Whom did Paul trust to meet his needs? In whom did Paul rejoice when the gift was received from the Philippians (verse 10)?

3. How do we accomplish God's purpose by supporting His servants? Read 1 Corinthians 9:14 and 1 Timothy 5:17.

Paul's commendation for the Philippians' gift was not a hint for another gift. Paul did not need gifts to rejoice. He did not need the Philippians' financial support in order to be content.

4. Why must real contentment come from within, not from external circumstances? Read 1 John 2:16 and 17.

"Contentment is having that spiritual artesian well within so that you don't have to run to the broken cisterns of the world to get what you need. The power of Christ in the inner man is all we need for the demands of life. Resources on the outside, such as friends and counselors and encourage-

> *ments, are only helpful as they strengthen our resources on the inside."[1]*

5. Contentment is not an instant decision (verse 11). How did Paul learn to be content? Read 1 Corinthians 4:11–13 and 2 Corinthians 9:8.

> *"Paul had been in God's school of discipline, and earned his advance degree by taking post-graduate courses in difficulty. Paul was a victor over every circumstance, not a victim to any circumstance. He adjusted well to the will of God."[2]*

6. How do we learn to be content? Read 1 Timothy 6:8 and Hebrews 13:5.

> *"The art of life consists in taking each event which befalls us with a contented mind, confident of good. This makes us grow younger as we grow older, for youth and joy come from the soul to the body more than from the body to the soul. With this method and art and temper of life, we live, though we may be dying. We rejoice always, though in the midst of sorrows; and possess all things, though destitute of everything."[3]*

7. The dictionary defines materialism as "the tendency to be more concerned with material than with spiritual or intellectual values." How does living in a materialistic society affect our contentment?

> Possessions weigh me down in life;
> I never feel quite free.
> I wonder if I own my things,
> Or if my things own me?

8. Read 1 Timothy 6:6–10. What reason did Paul give Timothy for being content (verse 7)? Read also Job 1:21.

9. With what should we be content (1 Timothy 6:8)?

10. What are the dangers of not being content with what we have (1 Timothy 6:9, 10)?

Paul said that he knew what it meant to be abased, or humbled, by poverty, and he knew what it was to abound, or overflow, in an abundance of prosperity (verse 12).

"The apostle . . . was initiated into that group of believers who learned to put their confidence in God, not gold. His faith in divine provision was not weakened by depression, recession, inflations, or affluence ('everywhere and in all things'). Food and money, in shortage or abundance, did not alter his spirituality."[4]

The power of God
Read Philippians 4:13.

11. Paul said he could do anything—handle poverty or wealth or whatever situation he faced (verse 13). What is the secret of such power?

"We exchange our strength for His strength. We hand in our little pocket batteries and plug into His dynamo! He has all the strength we need to keep going. . . ."[5]

---

12. Does "all things" suggest a sense of omnipotence? Does it mean we can do anything and everything? Explain your answer.

"When Paul says all things, *does he literally mean all things? Does it mean you can go outside and jump over your house? Of course not. Paul says, 'I can do all things in Christ'—that is, in the context of the will of Christ for your life. Whatever Christ has for you to do, He will supply the power. Whatever gift He gives you, He will give the power to exercise that gift."*[6]

---

13. Why do some people fail in what they want to do for Christ? Read John 15:5.

14. How can we avail ourselves of the power Paul had that enabled him to be content in every situation? Read Ephesians 1:15–20.

The provision of God
Read Philippians 4:14–19.

When Paul left Philippi and continued the second missionary journey, the church at Philippi was the only church helping him financially (verse 15). While he was in Thessalonica, the Philippians sent two gifts for his support (verse 16). Paul had mentioned these gifts when he wrote to the Corinthians (2 Corinthians 8:1–3; 11:9). Paul was more concerned about what giving did for the Philippians than he was in the need it met in his life. Their generosity would go down in the eternal records ("abound to your account," verse 17) of the deeds done in the flesh (2 Corinthians 5:10).

"The one who furnishes means of support has a part with the one who goes forth proclaiming the gospel of salvation. Every army is dependent upon its lines of supply. God has His supply troops who loyally stand behind the missionaries of the cross, upholding them in prayer before God and sacrificially giving money to pay expenses."[7]

15. What was the "fruit" that would be credited to the Philippians' account (verse 17)? Read John 15:16.

16. Why was the Philippians' gift a sacrifice to God (verse 18)? Read Hebrews 13:16 ("communicate" means "share").

17. Because Paul knew the people had sacrificed for him, what encouragement did he share with them (verse 19)?

18. What prerequisites should we put on the promise of Philippians 4:19? Read Matthew 6:31–33 and 2 Corinthians 8:1–5.

"Where God guides He provides. He is responsible for our upkeep if we follow His directions. He is not responsible for expenses not on His schedule. He does not foot the bill when we leave His itinerary."[8]

19. God promises to meet our needs—not our wishes, whims, and wants. What needs, other than financial, will Christ supply in our lives?

Benediction
Read Philippians 4:20–23.

Paul closed the book with a final greeting from himself, his fellow workers, and other believers in Caesar's household whom he had led to Christ while there in prison.

20. With what blessing did Paul close his letter?

Now that you have completed this study, here is a summary of principles from the book of Philippians that will help you joyously journey through life regardless of the detours:
- Remember that God is still working on you (1:6).
- Accept suffering for Christ's sake with joy (1:29).
- Live in harmony with fellow believers (2:2–4).
- Do not murmur and complain (2:14).
- Seek to know Christ better (3:10).
- Keep focused on the goal (3:14).
- Worry about nothing; pray about everything (4:6, 7).
- Think right thoughts (4:8).
- Learn to be content (4:11).
- Appropriate Christ's strength to do His will (4:13).

 From My Heart

Life was a joyous journey for Paul, in spite of the fact it was filled with detours. It can be the same for us! Yes, we can learn to joyously journey around the detours of life and experience peace and contentment while we're doing it.

It took me almost a year to write this study, and during that time I had to adjust to many varied experiences. Many times I had to remember, "Adjust or self-destruct." I have had to live out almost every lesson in one way or another as I have written the study. Often when I sat down to write, I'd say, "Lord, how can I write about joy with these painful circumstances surrounding me?" One day I came across the following quotation, and it lifted my spirits and got my eyes off myself and back on the Lord: "I know it has seemed like a long journey, but it will be shorter if you will keep this in mind: you aren't supposed to feel satisfied where you are. This isn't home. This is travel. Meantime, why not enjoy the scenery? You will never pass this way again and one day you will cherish the memories of this trip, if you will take note of them now. Otherwise, you might arrive at point 'B' with no stories to tell!"[9]

The following story will encourage you as you seek to joyously journey around the detours of life.

The Bike Ride

At first I saw God as my observer, my judge, keeping track of what I did. I recognized His picture, but really didn't know Him. But later on when I met Christ, it seemed as though life were rather like a bike ride; but it was a tandem bike, and I noticed that Christ was in the back helping me pedal.

I . . . know just when it happened that He suggested we change places. . . . Life has not been the same since. . . .

When I had control, I knew the way. It was rather boring, but predictable. . . . It was the shortest distance between two points. But when He took the lead, He knew delightful long cuts, up mountains, and through rocky places and at breakneck speeds. It was all I could do to hold on! Even though it looked like madness, He said, "Pedal."

I was worried and anxious and asked, "Where are you taking me?" He laughed and didn't answer, and I started to learn to trust. I forgot my boring life and entered the adventure. And when I'd say, "I'm scared," He'd lean back and touch my hand.

He took me to people with gifts that I needed, gifts of . . . acceptance and joy. They gave me their gifts to take on my journey, our journey, my Lord's and mine, and we were off again. He said, "Give the gifts away; they're extra baggage, too much weight."

So I did to the people we met, and I found that in giving I received, and still our burden was light. I did not trust Him at first, in control of my life. I thought He would wreck it; but He knows bike secrets, knows how to make it bend to take sharp corners, jump to clear high rocks, fly to shorten scary passages.

I am learning to shut up and pedal in the strangest

places, and I am beginning to enjoy the view and the cool breeze on my face, with my delightful constant companion, Christ. And when I am sure I just can't do any more, He just smiles and says, "Pedal."[10]

From Your Heart

What robs you of joy in your life? What causes you to be discontent? How will this study of Philippians help you make the necessary changes so you can have a joyous journey?

Perhaps our paths will meet someday in this journey down here. If not, I'll see you up there!

Juanita

Notes

1. Warren W. Wiersbe, *The Bumps Are What You Climb On* (Grand Rapids: Baker Book House, 1980), p. 132.

2. Edward E. Hindson and Woodrow M. Kroll, eds., *Liberty Commentary on the New Testament* (Lynchburg, Va.: Liberty Press, 1978), p. 553.

3. James Freeman Clarke, quoted by Tileston, p. 180.

4. Gromacki, p. 187.

5. Wiersbe, *The Bumps Are What You Climb On,* p. 77.

6. McGee, p. 327.

7. Alfred Martin, *Rejoicing in Christ* (Chicago: Moody Bible Institute, 1963), p. 26.

8. Havner, p. 75.

9. Slagle, p. 37.

10. Source unknown.

LEADER'S
GUIDE

SUGGESTIONS FOR LEADERS

The effectiveness of a group Bible study usually depends on two things: (1) the leader herself and (2) the ladies' commitment to prepare beforehand and interact during the study. You cannot totally control the second factor, but you have total control over the first one. These brief suggestions will help you be an effective Bible study leader.

You will want to prepare each lesson a week in advance. During the week, read supplemental material and look for illustrations in the everyday events of your life as well as in the lives of others. The following books may be helpful to you in your study:

Be Joyful by Warren W. Wiersbe (Victor Books, Wheaton, Ill.).

Bound for Joy by Stuart Briscoe (G/L Publications, Glendale, Calif.).

Devotional Studies in Philippians by Lehman Strauss (Loizeaux Brothers, Nepture, N.J.).

Philippians: Triumph in Christ by John F. Walvoord (Moody Press, Chicago).

Stand United in Joy by Robert Gromacki (Baker Book House, Grand Rapids).

The Bible Knowledge Commentary: New Testament Edition by John F. Walvoord and Roy B. Zuck, eds. (Victor Books, Wheaton, Ill.).

The Joy of Living by J. Dwight Pentecost (Zondervan Publishing House, Grand Rapids).

Encourage the ladies in the Bible study to complete each lesson before the meeting itself. This preparation will make the discussion more interesting. You can suggest that ladies answer two or three questions a day as part of their daily Bible reading time rather than trying to do the entire lesson at one sitting.

You may also want to encourage the ladies to memorize the key verse for each lesson. (This is the verse that is printed in italics at the start of each lesson.) If possible, print the verses on 3" x 5" cards to distribute each week. (Ask someone with a computer to make the cards for you if you cannot do it yourself.) If you cannot provide printed cards, suggest that the ladies make their own cards and keep them in a prominent place throughout the week.

The physical setting in which you meet will have some bearing on the study itself. An informal circle of chairs, chairs around a table, someone's living room or family room—these types of settings encourage people to relax and participate. In addition to an informal setting, create an atmosphere in which ladies feel free to participate and be themselves.

During the discussion time, here are a few things to observe.

• Don't do all the talking. This study is not designed to be a lecture.

• Encourage discussion on each question by adding ideas and questions.

• Don't discuss controversial issues that will divide the group. (Differences of opinion are healthy; divisions are not.)

• Don't allow one lady to dominate the discussion. Use statements such as these to draw others into the study: "Let's hear from someone on this side of the room" (the side opposite the dominant talker); "Let's hear from someone who has not shared yet today."

• Stay on the subject. The tendency toward tangents is always possible in a discussion. One of your responsibilities as the leader is to keep the group on the track.

• Don't get bogged down on a question that interests only one person.

You may want to use the last fifteen minutes of the scheduled time for prayer. If you have a large group of ladies, divide into smaller groups for prayer. You could call this the "Share and Care Time."

If you have a morning Bible study, encourage the ladies to go out for lunch with someone else from time to time. This is a good way to get acquainted with new ladies. Occasionally you could plan a time when ladies bring their own lunches or salads to share and have lunch together. These things help promote fellowship and friendship in the group.

The formats that follow are suggestions only. You can plan your own format, use one of these, or adapt one of these to your needs.

2-hour Bible Study

10:00—10:15 Coffee and fellowship time
10:15—10:30 Get-acquainted time
             Have two ladies take five minutes each to tell some-
             thing about themselves and their families.
             Also use this time to make announcements and, if ap-
             propriate, take an offering for the babysitters.
10:30—11:45 Bible study
             Leader guides discussion of the questions in the day's
             lesson.
11:45—12:00 Prayer time

2-hour Bible Study

10:00—10:45 Bible lesson
             Leader teaches a lesson on the content of the material.
             No discussion during this time.
10:45—11:00 Coffee and fellowship
11:00—11:45 Discussion time
             Divide into small groups with an appointed leader for
             each group. Discuss the questions in the day's lesson.
11:45—12:00 Prayer time

1¹/₂-hour Bible Study

10:00—10:30 Bible study
             Leader guides discussion of half the questions in the
             day's lesson.
10:30—10:45 Coffee and fellowship
10:45—11:15 Bible study
             Leader continues discussion of the questions in the
             day's lesson.
11:15—11:30 Prayer time

ANSWERS FOR LEADER'S USE

Information inside parentheses ( ) is instruction for the group leader.

LESSON 1

1. Saul.
2. The stoning of Stephen.
3. Saul's commitment in life was to kill Christians and destroy the church.
4. Jesus Christ revealed Himself to Saul on the road to Damascus, and Saul's life was transformed.
5. (Ask a few ladies to share their experiences.)
6. "Saul, Saul, why persecutest thou me? it is hard for thee to kick against the pricks."
7. Saul was blind. He was led by his companions into Damascus. He was blind for three days and did not eat or drink during that time.
8. Go to Saul and lay hands on him so he could receive his sight.
9. Ananias had heard that Saul had persecuted the Christians in Jerusalem and that he intended to arrest believers in Damascus.
10. One illustration is witnessing to an antagonistic relative or employer. We are afraid of how the person will react, what she might say, and how we will handle the situation.
11. The Lord told Ananias He had chosen Saul to take the message of salvation to Gentiles, kings, and the people of Israel. God also told Ananias that Saul would suffer for His name's sake.
12. Instantly Saul could see. He was filled with the Holy Spirit, and he was baptized.
13. They are the church of God, sanctified in Christ Jesus, and called to be saints.
14. "Them that believe."
15. A saint is a person who has believed on the Lord Jesus for salvation and, as a result, has been set apart by God for His holy purpose.
16. (Ask several ladies to share their testimonies.)

LESSON 2

1. Timothy was with Paul and Silas in Philippi on the second missionary journey and knew the believers there. Then he was with Paul in Rome. Timothy was Paul's fellow servant, but not a co-writer of the book.
2. Pastors.
3. You can learn to be content if you want to be. But you cannot do this in your own strength. You must avail yourself of God's strength.
4. The salvation of Lydia and her family and the jailer and his family, and the church that was established as a result.
5. (a) Joy. (b) He didn't have his mind on his present circumstances. His mind was rehearsing God's blessings in his life.
6. The Philippians helped Paul financially at least twice.

7. God will finish the work He begins in a person's life.

8. When we walk by sight rather than faith, we want to understand everything God is doing in our lives and in the lives of others. When we develop confidence in God, we say, "God is in control. I can't change what He controls, but I can trust the One Who is in control."

9. Circumstances: fear of the future and guilt about the past. People: We can let the behavior of other people fill us with bitterness, anger, and resentment. Things: We may become covetous of other people's things or overwork to have more things of our own.

10. Both verses refer to the beginning of new life in Christ. The Holy Spirit is the One Who creates within us a need for God and opens our eyes to see the real meaning of Christ and the cross.

11. His Son.

12. Until the day of Jesus Christ.

13. The event known as the "Rapture," described in 1 Thessalonians 4:16–18. When we are caught up to meet the Lord in the air, we shall be like Him, for we shall see Him as He is.

14. Once God begins His work in a life, He will not give up. The Lord loves His child and will chasten her, if necessary, to bring her back to Himself. (See Hebrews 12:6–11.)

15. Closeness, love, and compassion.

16. Jesus Christ.

17. *Verse 9*—He prayed that their love would keep growing for one another and that they would use good knowledge and discernment in showing this love to one another. *Verse 10*—He prayed that they would put a high priority on the best things in life so they could stand before Christ blameless on the judgment day. *Verse 11*—He prayed that their lives would be filled with evidence of right living so that they would bring honor and praise to Christ.

18. Love is the first fruit of the Spirit; without love all the other fruits lose their luster. Love is the greatest of the three great virtues (faith, hope, and love).

19. (No answers are necessary.)

LESSON 3

1. More people were hearing the gospel, even the palace guards. A guard was chained to Paul twenty-four hours a day. The guards changed every six hours, so four men were Paul's captive audience each day.

2. His courage and boldness were contagious. He stimulated new zeal in other believers to share Christ. Fear of persecution no longer overwhelmed the believers.

3. They were not preaching sincerely. Instead, they were trying to add to Paul's suffering.

4. He rejoiced that the message of Christ was being preached.

5. (a) We are usually defensive and self-protective. (b) Love our enemies, bless them that curse us, do good to those who hate us, and pray for those who persecute us.

6. Paul expected to be released from prison. He believed the Philippians' prayers for him would be answered in this regard.

7. (Have ladies share their experiences.)

8. That Christ would be magnified in his body.

9. (a) He would make Christ look large, or great, in the eyes of others. A distant Christ would be brought close. (b) If we seek to glorify Christ in all we do, we will be magnifying Him to a watching world.

10. I call this "palms-up living." It is turning loose of everything and trusting God completely. For more thoughts on living the palms-up life, see pages 36–41 in *Trials—Don't Resent Them as Intruders* (Schaumburg, Ill.: Regular Baptist Press).

11. (Some ladies may be willing to share their answers.)

12. His entire life was wrapped up in Christ. Christ lived in him, and he lived for Christ.

13. He would be in Christ's presence.

14. (Ask the ladies to honestly evaluate their lives.)

15. When we die, we will leave behind any other thing or person around which life revolves. We don't take anything with us to Heaven except the treasures we have already stored up there. If we are not living for Christ, we will be ashamed to see Him.

16. To die and be with Christ or to stay on earth and continue his ministry.

17. He would be with Christ, and that was far better than any earthly circumstance.

18. They fear the process of dying, the pain and suffering. If they are not living for the Lord, they fear facing Him.

19. God still had a job for him to do.

20. (Ask one or two ladies to share their answers.)

LESSON 4

1. (Many answers are possible; ask the ladies to share some. Be sure the list includes things such as gossip, bitterness, and a rebellious spirit, as well as the more obvious things such as adultery or other sinful lifestyles.)

2. That they were striving together with one mind and spirit for the advance of the gospel.

3. It takes self-discipline to be persistent day after day. Persistence is the constant challenge involved in living a Christlike life.

4. God always sees us. This fact should motivate us to live to please Him at all times.

5. *1 Corinthians 16:13*—Be steadfast in the faith. *Galatians 5:1*—Be steadfast in Christian liberty. *2 Thessalonians 2:15*—Be steadfast in the teachings of Scripture.

6. (a) Terrify us and fill us with fear. (b) The Devil.

7. The Victor, Jesus Christ, is praying for them, causing them to be victorious. In addition, nothing—no adversary—can separate believers from Christ.

8. Suffering for Christ's sake.

9. Many trials in this life cause us pain and suffering, such as divorce, rebellious children, broken health. But suffering for Christ's sake is being persecuted, ridiculed, or forsaken because of our faith in Christ.

10. The beating and imprisonment in Philippi.

11. (1) Since you have experienced the consolation, or gentle encouragement, of the Lord, be of one mind. (2) Since you have experienced the comforting love of Christ, be of one mind. (3) Since you are indwelt by the same Holy Spirit as other believers, be of one mind. (4) Since you know and have experienced in your heart the kindness and mercy of Christ, be of one mind. ("Bowels" were considered the seat of the emotions.)

12. Be like-minded.

13. Love, one accord, one mind.

14. Being one in spirit and purpose. It does not mean we never have differing views or opinions.

15. Strife and vainglory.

16. *Strife*—Bitter or violent conflict or dissention; contention for superiority. This causes discord because both sides feel they are right. Often a spirit of despising or envy is the basis for strife. *Vainglory*—Pride or conceit because of one's accomplishments. Pride causes discord because the big "I" takes over: "I demand my rights!" "I know I'm right!" "Why should I have to take this?"

17. (1) Humbly consider others better than yourself and submit to one another. (2) Look not only on your own interests but also consider the interests of others. Live to please others, not yourself.

18. A Biblical view of self puts others and their interests before myself and my interests. It is a servant mind-set, humbling myself to serve others.

LESSON 5

1. Lowliness of mind; thinking of others instead of ourselves.

2. He was willing to leave all the glories of Heaven to come into an ugly, sinful world, full of ugly, sinful people. While He was here on earth, He served these unappreciative, hateful people and eventually died for them.

3. Christ didn't grasp His own things; He looked, instead, on the sinful plight of others.

4. He gave up the glory of the Father's face for the muck of the earth, the adoration of angels for men to spit in His face. (Other things may also be mentioned.)

5. When He was born in Bethlehem; at the Incarnation.

6. We must daily deny our selfish desires and whims and put them to death on the cross of God's will. We are ready, then, to follow His will instead of our will.

7. A servant.

8. (Ask the ladies to examine themselves. Ask for volunteers to share their thoughts on servitude.)

9. Christ set the example of One Who ministered to the needs of others. The person with a Christlike attitude will ask, "What can I do for you?" not, "What can you do for me?"

10. He washed their feet.

11. To serve each other (wash each other's feet).

12. To be willing to minister to the needs of others, regardless of how lowly the service may be.

13. Some examples are working in the church nursery, serving in the kitchen, ministering to shut-ins, doing janitorial work.

14. Most of us would not be pleased at such a request. The only way we could do it would be to think about that person the way Christ would. Then we must think about ourselves in the role of servant just as Christ was.

15. Not being willing to consider other people better than ourselves. We don't want to humble ourselves; we want other people to be humble.

16. He submitted to death by crucifixion, an accursed way to die (Deut. 21:23; Gal. 3:13).

17. (a) She will allow Him to do what He wants in her life. She will be as clay in the potter's hands. (b) She will not think of herself more highly than she should; she will recognize that all she has comes from God. (c) She will put the needs and interests of others ahead of her own.

18. When we exalt ourselves by self-promotion, it may be temporary and can be embarrassing when we are asked to step down. God has His own unique way of making known the achievements of the humble person.

19. God exalted Christ and gave Him a name above every other name.

20. One day every person, saved and unsaved, will bow before Christ and acknowledge that He is Jesus Christ the Lord.

LESSON 6

1. The example of Christ.

2. Salvation is not something we earn or achieve as a result of our own efforts and striving. Salvation is a gift of God, started by God before the foundation of the world (Eph. 1:4). His Holy Spirit takes up residence in us when we accept Christ as Savior and begins to work in us to change us into the likeness of Jesus Christ (Rom. 8:29).

3. The Philippians were to work out in practical living the salvation that God had already worked in them.

4. (a) His work is to conform us to the image of His Son. (b) Our work is to place ourselves in His hands so He can transform us. God works in our hearts, giving us the desire to please Him. He also gives us the power to carry out His desire. Our work is to surrender to His will in complete obedience.

5. With fear and trembling, meaning reverence and a healthy respect for God.

6. A healthy awe and respect for God will cause us to want to please Him.

7. God works in us. He wants us to grow, so He just keeps nudging us forward.

8. God energizes us inwardly so we will want to do His will.

9. (a) (Ask for volunteers to share their experiences.) (b) God had to work in Moses for forty years in the desert before He could work through him to lead the Children of Israel. God worked on Jonah in the big fish. God worked on Paul for three years in the Arabian desert.

10. His good pleasure—what pleases Him.

11. Without murmurings and disputings.

12. *Murmuring*—Grumbling, complaining, whining, a discontented spirit. This can be done alone or with others. *Disputing*—Verbal expressions of disagreement that could stir up distrust and disturbing feelings in others.

13. (a) The Children of Israel when they rejected the report of the two spies and refused to enter Canaan. (b) He said the people would die in the wilderness because they had murmured against Him and doubted Him. (c) No.

14. They complain about the circumstances God has allowed. Their complaining shows they doubt God's goodness to them. This can cause others to dispute against God and doubt Him. Sometimes people murmur and complain against God's servants and rebel against their leadership as the Children of Israel did against Moses.

15. Their lives will be blameless, harmless, and without rebuke.

16. They bring reproach on the name of Christ and are looked upon as hypocrites.

17. As lights.

18. People will see our good works and glorify God.

19. He didn't want to be ashamed when he stood before Christ. He wanted to know that his life and labors were not in vain.

20. Paul regarded this as a spiritual experience (a sacrifice) and anticipated it with joy. His thinking may have been something like this, "Even if this imprisonment is my last experience on earth, I will still rejoice, and I want you to rejoice as well. God has been so faithful to me, and now Heaven is closer."

21. Rejoice with him.

LESSON 7

1. He was sending Timothy to find out the Philippians' "state" (i.e., how they had responded to Paul's teachings in this letter).

2. So he would be comforted.

3. He hoped to hear that the Philippians were getting along better with each other. Their spiritual growth would encourage the apostle.

4. (Ask the ladies to share their experiences.)

5. Timothy was like-minded with Paul and would care for the Philippians just as Paul would have.

6. By our interest in them, our involvement with them, and our investment of time and possessions, if need be.

7. Paul practiced what he preached.

8. To understand each other's motives and needs; to think alike; to need no explanation.

9. They were like father and son, serving together in the cause of Christ.

10. Paul was Timothy's spiritual father. Paul had led Timothy to Christ when Paul visited Lystra on the second missionary journey. Timothy continued on the journey with Paul and Silas.

11. Timothy was there when the church in Philippi was started. He visited Philippi on three other occasions.

12. Paul waited to see how things were going to go for him in prison and how soon he would be released. Timothy could then give the Philippians a report on Paul's situation.

13. The Philippian church had sent him to Rome to deliver a financial gift to Paul.

14. (a) "My brother," "companion in labour," "fellowsoldier." (b) Brother—bound by love; companion in labor—bound by service; fellow soldier—bound by common danger and heartaches.

15. He became very ill and almost died.

16. He was distressed because the Philippians had heard about his illness.

17. (a) So that Paul's sorrows would not be increased. (b) God knows how much we can bear. In His mercy, He does not give us more than our "frame" can endure.

18. So the Philippians could rejoice in seeing him alive and well again.

19. Paul would have joy because he knew the Philippians were rejoicing.

20. Because he had risked his life for the work of Christ. He was at the point of death trying to do things for Paul because the Philippians were too far away to help.

21. (No answers are necessary.)

22. The Lord Jesus Christ.

LESSON 8

1. Paul wanted the Philippians to remember what Christ had done for them. Also, he may have wanted to start this part of the letter in a positive way.

2. (a) Repetition is vital to learning. (b) Possible ways to keep oneself reminded include be accountable to someone, review Scripture, write notes to yourself.

3. God now requires circumcision of the heart.

4. He wanted the Philippians to realize how serious false teaching is.

5. (Have the ladies share some of their experiences.)

6. (1) He worships God in the Spirit. He worships God because of love, not law. This love is inspired and guided by the Holy Spirit, Who lives in him. (2) He rejoices or boasts in Christ. He is continually praising Christ and telling others what a great Savior he has. (3) He has no confidence in the flesh. He doesn't boast about what he is doing for Christ but in what Christ has done and is doing in his life.

7. They try to earn Heaven by good works, by keeping the ordinances or sacraments of the church, by being baptized, by giving money. (Other answers are also possible.)

8. Our salvation is gained by trusting what Christ did for us on the cross, not by trusting in what we can do for ourselves. Anything we do in the flesh ("our righteousnesses") are as filthy rags in God's sight.

9. *Pride of race*—He was a pure-blooded Jew, circumcised the eighth day. (Proselytes were circumcised later in life; Ishmaelites after age thirteen.) Both of his parents were Jews. He could trace his lineage back

to Abraham. *Pride of family*—He was a Benjamite, the tribe from which Israel's first king came. *Pride of religion*—He was a Pharisee, the strictest sect of the Jews. He kept hundreds of laws. *Pride of zeal*—He persecuted people who weren't Jews, the church. *Pride of morality*—In his legalistic righteousness, Paul considered himself blameless.

10. He counted it all as loss.

11. (You may want to ask a lady ahead of time to share a brief testimony of the change in her life.)

12. He felt he had gained far more than he had lost. Knowing Christ as His Savior far surpassed all the religious performances he was involved in. He looked at everything before his salvation as worthless garbage ("dung").

13. Christ alone.

14. *Romans 3:12; 4:5*—Righteousness is received by faith in Christ. *1 Corinthians 1:30*—Jesus Christ is our righteousness. *2 Corinthians 5:21*—We can be made righteous because Christ was made sin.

15. (a) By spending time with the person. (b) By spending time with Him and reading His Word.

16. The power of Christ's resurrection and the fellowship of His sufferings.

17. We will have the power to turn our backs on sin and have boldness in speaking to others about Christ. We also will have the power to accept whatever God sends, even suffering, without complaining against Him.

18. We must count ourselves as dead to sin and alive to God. We must learn to walk in the Spirit, which means to be controlled by Him instead of by our selfish desires and motives.

19. Accept the suffering with joy.

20. The Lord Himself will help you because He has been through all this ahead of you, and He will see you safely through.

21. Die daily to self. Our daily prayer must be, "Not my will but Thy will be done."

22. (Have volunteers share their answers.)

LESSON 9

1. He said he had not attained the goals he set forth in verse 10. He was not perfect yet; he still failed to live up to God's standards.

2. Christians sin because they still have an old nature, a "law" present within them that is bent to do evil.

3. To reveal His Son in Paul to people who were in the darkness of sin.

4. To make us into the image of His Son.

5. (No answer is required.)

6. I'm not there yet. I haven't captured the prize for which I'm running.

7. He forgot the past and kept his eye on the goal in front of him.

8. The Lord Jesus.

9. (Ask volunteers to share their answers.)

10. Failures can cause us to develop a selfish, poor-me spirit. This spirit can lead to discouragement and may cause us to drop out of the race.

11. If Christ is willing to forgive and forget, we must forgive and forget and move on.

12. He is not fit to be a disciple.

13. In addition to forgetting the past, we need to lay aside anything that will hinder us from running well.

14. (Some ladies may be willing to share their answers.)

15. "Press toward the mark."

16. (a) "The high calling of God in Christ Jesus." (b) Incorruptible, or imperishable.

17. He did not run with uncertainty. He disciplined himself and ran with purpose.

18. The example of Jesus Christ.

19. He had finished the race.

20. When we see Christ, we will be like Him.

21. Have this same goal for your lives—Christlikeness.

LESSON 10

1. (a) Salvation (they were saints). (b) Live like saints.

2. In the way he followed Christ.

3. Timothy and Epaphroditus.

4. (Ask the ladies to share their answers.)

5. The Christian faith is not just for Bible characters. To see that same faith practiced and lived out in the lives of others who face the same struggles we face gives us hope that we can live that way as well.

6. The people around us.

7. He was weeping.

8. They were under divine judgment. Their end would be destruction.

9. As apostles of Christ and ministers of righteousness.

10. An increase in false teachers and their popularity.

11. Mormonism, Seventh-day Adventism, Jehovah's Witnesses; other answers may also be given.

12. Brokenhearted as Paul was.

13. Their end is destruction; their god is their belly; their glory is their shame; they mind earthly things.

14. Their goal is to please self and gratify their selfish desires, or appetites.

15. Temporal things. This lifestyle is often summarized in the philosophy that says, "Eat, drink and be merry, for tomorrow we die."

16. She should keep her mind fixed on heavenly things.

17. (No answers are needed.)

18. Conduct or citizenship.

19. Paul and Peter both referred to believers as strangers and foreigners here.

20. When He appears at the Rapture. (The word "Rapture" means "caught up," as pictured in 1 Thessalonians 4:17.)

21. We shall be changed into incorruptible beings. We will receive glorified bodies.

22. Like Christ's body after the Resurrection. He ascended into Heaven in that body (Acts 1:11).

23. Christ will be the supreme ruler. All His enemies will be destroyed.

24. They will appear before God at the Great White Throne Judgment.

Because their names are not in the Book of Life, they will be cast into the Lake of Fire.

LESSON 11

1. (a) Stay steady. (b) He had just described false teachers. He wanted the Philippians to keep holding to the teaching of Christ as they always had and not be swayed by the teachings and traditions of men.

2. (a) "In the Lord." (b) Verse 1—We should stand firm in Him. Verse 2—We can have unity through Him. Verse 4—He is our reason for rejoicing.

3. Be like-minded.

4. They usually go to one extreme or the other: they won't speak to each other, or they fuss and argue.

5. They had labored with him in the gospel. They had been involved in his ministry in Philippi and were probably "charter members" of the Philippian church.

6. *Romans 5:2*—Rejoice because you have been justified and have hope for the future. *Romans 15:13*—Rejoice because of your belief in Christ. *1 Thessalonians 2:19, 20*—Rejoice in the ministry you can have in other people's lives. *1 Peter 1:8*—Rejoice because you belong to Christ.

7. We will have strength and energy to do God's work.

8. Unselfishness, forbearance, not easily offended, sweet reasonableness, gentleness. The word comes from the verb "yield," meaning we won't demand our rights.

9. One example is the checkout line in the supermarket. You are in the line marked cash only and ten items or less; the lady in front of you has twenty items and wants to write a check. The natural response is to sigh and make an unkind remark to the person behind you.

10. The return of Christ.

11. We will be obedient to His commands because we want to be found faithful and not ashamed when He returns.

12. Food, clothing, the future.

13. We need to realize we are not adequate in ourselves.

14. He is sufficient for all things.

15. Let our requests be made known to God.

16. Sustain us (carry us and our burdens).

17. The peace of God.

18. It keeps us stable by building a wall around our hearts and minds to keep out worrisome thoughts. ("Keep" is a military term that means "garrison" or "guard.")

19. *True*—This is the opposite of lies and false witness. A truthful life (Eph. 5:9) will promote joy and peace. *Honest*—Think about and live a life of integrity (2 Cor. 8:21). *Just*—Think about things that measure up to God's standards. *Pure*—Don't fill your mind with the immoral world of soaps and cinema. We have to be clean inwardly to have inward peace (James 3:17). *Lovely*—Think about things that bring pleasure and joy. *Good report*—Think about things that have essential worthiness (1 Cor. 13:6). Don't dwell on people's failures and weaknesses; think about their good traits (1 Cor. 13:7).

20. (a) Television, videos, movies, magazines and books, comtemporary music. Other answers are possible. (b) God's Word.
21. Obey what we have been taught.

LESSON 12

1. No.
2. God.
3. It is God's plan that His servants be supported by His people.
4. The things of the world will never bring contentment because they are temporal; they will pass away.
5. He went through many different circumstances and learned—over time and through these trials—that Christ is sufficient.
6. The more we grow in Christ, the more content we are with whatever He allows us to have and the less we need the world's toys, gadgets, and gold to be satisfied and happy.
7. The more we get, the more we want. Advertisers try to convince us that we simply cannot be happy unless we have their products. We bite the bait, and all we end up with is more things. These things can't bring contentment.
8. We came into the world with nothing, and we will leave with nothing.
9. Basic needs.
10. Trying to obtain material things may lead to sorrow and even to sin.
11. The indwelling Christ empowered him and enabled him to endure difficult outward circumstances.
12. No. We can do all the things we ought to do, not necessarily all the things we want to do. If I didn't know how to swim, it would be foolish of me to jump into a pool and expect God to let me swim. With God's strength I can do everything God requires of me.
13. They try to do it in their own strength, not relying on Christ.
14. God supplies the power in answer to prayer.
15. The Philippians had a part in the ministry of Paul. Paul's converts were, in a sense, their converts as well.
16. They gave as spiritual priests unto God.
17. "My God shall supply all your need."
18. Christ must be central in our lives; we must be seeking first His righteousness. This priority will involve giving ourselves and our substance to Him.
19. Physical, emotional, spiritual. Contentment can be ours because we know we have adequate resources available to us. He owns everything and wants to share His resources with us.
20. The prayer that God's grace (His unmerited favor) would continue with the readers of his letter.

Lovin

arents + school kids